JOHN ROSSELLI

Music & Musicians
IN NINETEENTH-CENTURY
Italy

JOHN ROSSELLI

Music & Musicians
IN NINETEENTH-CENTURY
Italy

B.T. Batsford Ltd · London

To the memory of
Viola and Giulio Michelotti,
with affection and gratitude

ISBN 0 7134 6153 5

Typeset by J&L Composition Ltd, Filey, North Yorkshire

and printed in Great Britain by
Biddles Ltd, Guildford

for the Publisher
B.T. Batsford Ltd
4 Fitzhardinge Street
London W1H 0AH

Contents

List of Illustrations

(*Between pages 96 and 97.*)

1. The tarantella. A somewhat idealized nineteenth-century lithograph, Museo di S. Martino, Naples (*Soprintendenza ai Beni Artistici e Storici, Naples*)

2. The apotheosis of the nineteenth-century Italian opera house: the Teatro Colón, Buenos Aires (1908), built and originally managed by Italians (*Teatro Colón*)

3. An all-Italian popular opera house overseas: the Teatro Marconi, Buenos Aires (1903; originally the Doria; destroyed *c.* 1960). The sign at the extreme right is that of the Gran Café Paganini (*Instituto de Estudios del Teatro, Buenos Aires*)

4. Giuditta Pasta as Anna Bolena in Donizetti's opera, 1830, by Brulo (*Museo Teatrale alla Scala, Milan*)

5a & b. Arnaldo Tedeschi in costume as Manrico in a children's opera company, *c.* 1904 (he did not sing the complete opera but appeared between the acts of comic operas to sing 'Di quella pira') (*Dr Guido A. Tedeschi*)

6. A product of local patriotism: a postcard showing the two leading tenors born in Montagnana, near Padua (Aureliano Pertile, left, as Nero in Boito's opera, Giovanni Martinelli, right, as Eléazar in Halévy's *La Juive*)

7. A setting for a romantic ballet: *Ettore Fieramosca*, Teatro San Carlo, 1837 (*Soprintendenza ai Beni Artistici e Storici, Naples*)

PART ONE

1 The Long Nineteenth Century

I sometimes sing in the street. To my English children 20 years ago this was matter for shame, even worse than the other oddities parents got up to. 'Daddy, don't sing!' they whispered. 'I'm a kind of Italian,' I would explain, 'and Italians sing in the street.' But even as I made this excuse it was ceasing to be true.

In Italy, television, the internal combustion engine and prosperity were putting an end to the old habit of living outside through the long warm months. The tape recorder was making it unnecessary to raise one's own voice in song; it was replacing semi-improvised melisma with the international language of rock-'n'-roll. Under the stars these nights in Naples you are more likely to hear a ghetto blaster than a plangent tenor.

The long nineteenth century began in Italy well before 1801 and went on well past 1900. Centuries are artificial units; in a fragmented, impoverished land and a deeply conservative society there was no clear break at the turn of the eighteenth and nineteenth centuries, even though the 1790s, bringing invasion by revolutionary French armies and then Napoleonic rule, did mark the beginnings of change at least in law and administration.

Much more than national unification in 1860 and more than fascism, the rapid industrialization of the last 35 years has been the great watershed. Shortly after the Second World War, half the Italian population still worked on the land, many of them at little more than subsistence level. In the 1990s the country ranks fifth among world economies, just ahead of Britain; the birthrate is the lowest in Western Europe; most people live in towns; most speak Italian instead of local dialects; the northern plain enjoys a West German level of widely diffused prosperity and, as Italians like to display their good fortune, this prosperity can be observed in clothes, cars and shopfittings as well, alas, as in an environment too much of it laid waste.

Change in history is uneven – in Italy above all. On the eve of the Second World War the daily lives of sharecropping or day-labouring peasants had changed little from a century or more earlier, save perhaps for the worse because of increased population and subsequent soil erosion. Many villages could still be reached only by mule tracks. Radio had come and occasionally there might be a travelling cinema, but many people were still illiterate and had little notion of the country beyond their parish except as an entity that demanded rents, taxes and military service. Cities such as Milan, Turin, Genoa, Bologna and Rome, however, had already in the last third of the nineteenth century developed modern business and residential areas, complete with trams, pompous institutional buildings, a white-collar and professional middle class and – in parts of the north only – the beginnings of an industrial working class. The long nineteenth century, then, came to an end at differing times in different parts of the country, with Milan and Turin in about 1870 already showing a modernity that was to elude the countryside and most of the south for at least six more decades.

In music too, there were time lags. The landless labourers who sat waiting for work in a Calabrian hill village in about 1950 could hear commercialized Neapolitan songs on the one radio in the place (kept in the bar); their womenfolk heard similar tunes on an accordion at the occasional horse fair on the mountainside; but all of them were still embedded in a traditional culture that made its own music, which was Arab-sounding and largely unrelated to music outside the region. The inhabitants of the big northern cities, on the other hand, were already, in the 1870s, beginning to follow international fashions in music – French initially but then German too: operetta, sentimental opera, Wagner, cabaret, even, very late, symphonic music – all these took root. Educated Italy became what it has been ever since, one of the most eclectic of nations, ready to absorb artistic and intellectual influences from all over the world.

This is curious, for the notion universally held for most of the eighteenth and nineteenth centuries was of Italy as the home of all the arts. It was, by definition, the land of song, the land of painters and sculptors and architects; of poets too, for in English-speaking countries Italian literature was thought particularly suitable for ladies. Like most clichés, this one had a kernel of truth: the sheer quantity of artistic production piled up in Italy over the centuries was and still is astonishing, much of it being of high technical excellence if nothing else.

In the nineteenth century this undeniable fact was mixed up in the minds of many people with romantic notions about the collective genius of the Italian people. Even the humblest Italians were supposed to have an inborn feeling for beauty. The art critic Roger Fry wrote that if you asked a Tuscan peasant to build you a barn he would come up with something in which door, window and roof-line stood in a seemingly inevitable harmonious relation to each other. Unfortunately, where we know the sources of Tuscan farm buildings of past centuries, they turn out to have been designed in Florence by professional architects whose models were then copied over and over. When, as in the past 30 years, Tuscan peasants have been able to build their own dwellings, they have perpetrated as much suburban ugliness as anyone else.

In music the notion of untutored Italian genius seems at first glance more plausible. Through most of the nineteenth century, visitors were again and again struck with the musical talents of the poor. The boy Mozart and his father, when in Milan in 1770, heard a beggar couple in the street sing a whole song in fifths without missing a note; something, Leopold Mozart wrote, that he had never heard in Germany. In the same year the British musicologist Charles Burney, on arrival at his inn in Venice, heard in the alley outside 'a band of musicians consisting of two good fiddles, a violoncello, and female voice, who performed in such a manner as would have made people stare in England, but here they were as little attended to as coalmen or oyster women are with us.' Nearly a century later, the French writer Hippolyte

Taine remarked in Naples on yet more street singers, whose voices were harsh but who sang in tune: 'they are real musicians, they understand shades of feeling, they know what is musically right and wrong ...'

Significantly, all these spontaneous musicians were heard in towns, and large towns at that. Although we know little about them as a group the chances are that they were somehow connected with the busy professional musical world of those towns, even though on its lowest rungs, as aspirants or failures. Peasants singing in the hills and fields were, as we shall see, virtually unheard for most of the nineteenth century, except by each other.

Part of the difficulty in hearing them was that at peasant level there was no such country as Italy. The land was divided, most obviously by the boundaries of the old Italian states. Until 1860 these meant passports and customs barriers – three on a journey from Florence to Parma of about 120 miles (200 km). But mountains, swamps and bad roads in many places were still greater obstacles. Historically, the countryside has been dominated and exploited, in most of north and central Italy by the old city states, elsewhere by the feudal nobility. Most peasants spoke a dialect fully understood only within a small region; when conscripted they often could not understand their fellow-soldiers or officers. Towns were intensely jealous of each other and might themselves be riven by fierce loyalties to neighbourhoods, something still found today in the notorious horse race at Siena.

For reasons of this kind, it has been said, only two per cent of Italians could speak Italian when the country was nominally unified in 1860 and few had any real sense of belonging to the new nation. This is to oversimplify. English people in particular, accustomed as they have been for centuries to a unified kingdom and a single language, are ill-equipped to understand the much more common situation of people who share an artistic and intellectual culture and some fundamental experiences but who do not necessarily all speak the same language or owe allegiance to the same state. Ancient Greece, India, Eastern Europe and the Iberian Peninsula are examples. So too in the old fragmented

Italy much of the urban population – admittedly a minority in the peninsula – could handle Italian, as well as the local dialect, for some purposes. They could also make something of two or three widely differing dialects: we can tell this from the way the popular *commedia dell'arte* – semi-improvised knockabout theatre – exploited stock characters who spoke Venetian, Bolognese, or Neapolitan; the same device was endlessly repeated in the popular comic operas of the eighteenth and early nineteenth centuries. But these shows embedded their dialect passages in an Italian text which audiences everywhere could understand.

So too the world of Italian art-music was highly unified. Whatever might be said of local schools, such as Naples or Venice, and the stylistic differences between them, the language of cultivated music in Italy, from the seventeenth to the nineteenth century, was essentially the same everywhere. The Sicilian Alessandro Scarlatti composed at different times for Naples, Rome and Florence; Galuppi's operas did as well in Naples and Turin as in his native Venice. When Rossini's works swept the country from 1813 his success was merely a more spectacular version of his predecessors'. These and most other composers travelled, taking new musical fashions with them; so too did singers and instrumentalists. Opera itself, the great Italian invention, had been spread in the mid-seventeenth century by travelling companies, so that experiments in Venice, Rome and Naples quickly merged into a single genre.

But musicians did not travel only in Italy. For this art, a musicologist wrote in 1774, the entire continent employed Italians as the Romans employed the Greeks: 'there is no corner of Europe so remote that you will not find there a few Italian singers and players; in our day they have even reached the East Indies …'. This was true of Europe certainly and of India probably. A mainly Italian comic opera company reached Moscow from Warsaw in the winter of 1730/1; it took a month and a half to go round by Kiev so as to avoid the wolf-infested marshes on the direct route, and was robbed of a chest of costumes along the way; on arrival the prima donna complained merely of the lack of chocolate. The Irish tenor Michael Kelly recalled having been taught in Dublin in the 1770s by three Italians in turn; he also mentioned the Italian leader of the opera orchestra and several other Italians who may have been musicians too. None of these people was famous. Star singers and leading composers did travel to London, Vienna, St Petersburg and Madrid, as well as to the capitals of the more important German princely states, generally with the intention of making money and then going home. Humbler musicians sometimes stayed on, so that in Russia during the eighteenth and early nineteenth centuries we come upon a failed impresario who opened a successful restaurant, and a woman singer who, after a career lasting 15 years, is last heard of in the provincial town of Zhitomir; no doubt she settled down and became a teacher.

Italy's folk music, then, was far too locally bounded to be Italian in any clear national sense; its art-music, on the other hand, fed an international market. Composers and performers, including Verdi and Puccini, Tetrazzini and Caruso, were eager to make both money and a reputation abroad, as was natural for hard-pressed musicians from a poor country. In that sense Italian music transcended Italy.

But this international vocation did not make such musicians or their art any less Italian. They remained Italian through and through, not because of nationalistic inclinations – the nationalism of the Italian musical world in this period has been greatly exaggerated – but because it scarcely occurred to them to speak, sing, play, or compose as other than Italians in an Italian idiom. Throughout the nineteenth century and beyond it has often been remarked how Italian musicians on their travels lived, ate, talked, and made music together, and how impermeable they were to the cultures they passed through. Composers and librettists might ransack the work of Sir Walter Scott and a dozen French playwrights, but it all had to go through the mill of Italian artistic convention. The great German soprano Lilli Lehmann sang not just Italian opera but, on occasion, Beethoven's *Fidelio* in Italian; it is virtually impossible to find an Italian artist who returned the compliment.

This essentially Italian character of the professional musical world held good even while musicians had to reckon with the courts, bureaucracies and local hierarchies of the nine, ten, or eleven petty states into which the peninsula was divided (the number of states fluctuated slightly according to the vicissitudes of European war and diplomacy, for Italy was used to being both a satellite and a battlefield for the great powers).

Professional musical life in the old Italy was focused on the capital cities of these petty states. Most of them were monarchies: this meant that if there was a permanent salaried orchestra it was most likely to be employed by the local ruler as part of his court establishment, and the same might be true of chorus singers and other opera house personnel. In the republics of Venice, Genoa, and Lucca (snuffed out by the French at the end of the eighteenth century), leading nobles were the patrons. This, however, made little difference, for in every Italian town, except the commercial ports of Leghorn and Trieste, the local nobility had a virtual monopoly of wealth and power, and even in a royal or ducal capital they staffed the more important government posts, put themselves on display in the boxes as the most prominent part of the audience at public performances, formed committees to run theatres and seasons, and still exercised a fraction of the private musical patronage they had enjoyed in the sixteenth and seventeenth centuries. In a city such as Bologna, at a distance from the capital (which happened to be Rome), the nobles who ran the municipality employed the permanent orchestra, and shared control of musical life with the cardinal legate who represented the pope.

Until the mid-eighteenth century the church had been at least as important a maker of music, whether through the patronage of cardinals in Rome or through the choirs and orchestras of cathedrals, monastic houses, pilgrimage churches, and other religious foundations. These were the days when in a deindustrialized country, monks and nuns made up as much as a tenth of the population of some of the sleepier central Italian towns, and oratorio, performed in churches, was at least as sought-after an entertainment as opera. But in the course of the eighteenth century the Church grew weaker, both in its claims to universal supremacy and in its hold on the allegiance of individuals. Roman Catholic sovereigns, among them some of the rulers of the Italian states, felt able to assert themselves by withholding some of the Church's privileges, confiscating some of its wealth, and suppressing some religious orders. Even in Italy a gradual change of outlook – the beginning of the move from a fundamentally religious to a fundamentally secular view of the world – was cutting down the number of monastic vocations. The popes had long had trouble reconciling their universal claims with looking after the interests of an Italian state. By the time Napoleon sent two successive popes into exile and made Rome his second capital the Papal States, though eventually restored, had dwindled into the creakiest and most conservative of petty principalities.

In these old Italian states music was understood to be the right thing for the great to patronize, whether, as individuals, they enjoyed it or not. The tie between royal or noble patrons on the one hand and musicians on the other was a personal one. It was a tie of protection and dependence, even though most musicians were no longer members of the great man's household, as they had been in renaissance times and for a while after.

At the beginning of the nineteenth century the King of Naples still kept up a rule forbidding all benefit performances, so that individual musicians would have to petition him to make an exception in their favour, as he often did. And this was a ruler who had no particular interest in music. If the great man did have such an interest, his involvement might be almost limitless. Thus, Cardinal Consalvi, the nearest thing to a reforming prime minister in the Papal States just after the overthrow of Napoleon, had a passion for the works of Cimarosa – already a rather old-fashioned taste – whose manuscripts he collected; he spent some of his time vetting opera librettos; his predecessor at one time exerted himself to remedy a shortage of bassoon players in Rome. King Charles Felix of Sardinia likewise vetted librettos and sought to control the distribution of arias and concerted pieces in particular works. Almost as a matter of routine, kings and dukes appealed to one another for help in securing the services of a tenor, and the Pope's envoy in Vienna took trouble to ensure that the famous ballerina Fanny Elssler appeared at a trade fair in the Papal States.

In this world of intense local feeling the 18 years of war and French rule that followed the invasion of 1796 marked something more than an interval. Napoleon drained the country ruthlessly of money and men; large numbers of Italians died as far afield as Russia. His wholesale redrawing of the map did not greatly disturb the local bigwigs; many served the new regime as they had the old. But his sweeping legal and administrative reforms did bring forward a new group of professional men, and the ceaseless wars took many men out of their old routines and gave them new glimpses of opportunities for change and command. All this was particularly true in Milan, which he made the capital of his kingdom of Italy (a misnomer, for it covered only part of the north and north-east).

The city developed an emergent middle class and a lively intellectual life. It also became the centre of Italian musical life. Like most things in Italy, musical life had until then been dispersed, with two or three chief centres and plenty of activity elsewhere. In the seventeenth and eighteenth centuries the chief nurseries of composers and performing musicians were first Rome and Venice, then Naples and, as a hive of teachers and a market-place for engagements, Bologna, conveniently placed at the crossroads of north and central Italy. Now Milan was to take first place in each of these roles; its leadership was symbolized in the one Italian opera house most people have heard of, La Scala.

In the country's musical life as a whole, the Napoleonic legacy was a matter of gradual but irreversible change in the social setting. Pre-revolutionary Italy had been dominated by royalty, nobility and their hangers on. At Parma only nobles were allowed candles in their theatre boxes, at Turin only noblewomen could have their way lighted by a torchbearer. At operas and public concerts the nobility were accompanied by hordes of liveried retainers, who often enjoyed free or cheap entry, prepared meals and drinks for their masters on the spot, and relieved themselves in the corridors. But, as a mark of their higher status, the nobles themselves generally paid more for admission than did 'citizens', that is middle-class townspeople, just as men generally paid more than women. The Napoleonic regime swept much of this finely graded hierarchy with its coarse underside away from La Scala. Elsewhere, the shift from lavish display to a more modern reticence took place gradually over the half-century leading up to unification. Some of the more expensive court musical establishments were cut back: the Turin royal orchestra, which had been one of the finest in eighteenth-century Europe, never fully recovered.

The period of French rule also brought in a new earnestness. Just as it meant continuous war after an unprecedented half-century of peace, so it bequeathed ideas of political liberty and economic efficiency. The pleasure-loving character of late-eighteenth-century Italy can be exaggerated – life had often been grim, especially for the poor – but, for the better off, places like Venice and Naples provided a refined luxury and a near endless round of entertainment, dominated in music by comic opera. Now that thinking people either sought revolution or feared it, comedy seemed out of place: it largely went out after a final burst of Rossinian fireworks. There were in fact attempted revolutions in parts of Italy between 1820 and 1821 and in 1831, and temporarily successful ones between 1848 and 1849.

Already in the French period, music had taken on new military qualities of attack, noise, and speed – to be heard in Rossini. Now, even in a country whose educated classes prided themselves on their inheritance of classical art – an art of impersonality and restraint, strong above all in formal qualities – music was to give voice to stronger passions.

2 The Roots of Musical Life

A characteristically Italian figure throughout the nineteenth century and down to the present is the singer who cannot read music. He or she is known as an *orecchiante*, literally 'earer'. A few have made great careers, for instance the soprano Brigida Banti, who flourished at the very end of the eighteenth century. Of her it was reported that 'she could not read a note of music, or a word of print, yet hearing an air once played over, and that but indifferently, she sang it most divinely'. She was also said to be bad-tempered and to drink a bottle of wine a day (but bottles were smaller then). Banti came of a poor family in a small town near Cremona, and began alongside her father as a street singer of the kind heard by Mozart and Burney.

Much later, in the 1930s, in another small town, this time inland from Venice, an impoverished shopkeeper's eight-year-old son called Gastone Limarilli would sometimes win a meal for his family when a friend's mother announced: 'I'll give five eggs to whoever sings the best high note'. He went on to a middling career as a tenor, and presumably grew out of the *orecchiante* stage even though he was dismissed from music school after four years. His story shows how, in quite recent times, an ordinary Italian – a housewife whose hens were laying well – could value musical accomplishment, even though at the rudimentary level of the loudest possible high C.

It is tempting to suppose that nineteenth-century professional musicians who sang or played by ear were peasants whose skill with pan-pipes, or whose voice raised in a folk song, had caught the attention of a passing expert. Tempting, but unlikely. The evidence suggests that professional musicians came from towns, many from within the profession itself. Folk music stayed with the folk. Peasants who sang and played remained peasants.

All over Europe, people discovered folk music as they discovered the pastness of the past; the notion that past society was unlike our own, and that ours has evolved out of it by an organic process of gradual change – summed up in the term 'historicism' – did not strike anybody until the seventeenth century. Towards the end of that century the first antiquarian collectors of folk music and folk song appeared; they were, for instance, interested in Welsh music, which (as they thought) had the prestige of being bound up with Ancient Britain and King Arthur. But although the Neapolitan writer Giambattista Vico was a pioneer of historicism, few Italians seem to have been interested in recording Italian folk music until very late in the nineteenth or early in the twentieth century, by which time the music itself had changed; fewer still refrained from embellishing it with 'correct' harmonies. We are therefore ill-informed. It is particularly difficult to imagine what tunes might have been heard in a Piedmontese ricefield or on a Sicilian fishing boat in about 1800; we know rather more of the words people sang and the instruments they used.

What is clear is that folk music differed widely from one part of Italy to another, so widely as to make the phrase 'Italian folk music' a catch-all. Southerners sang in a tense, high-pitched voice, mostly solo melodies in free rhythm, generally modal and related to Spanish and Arab song, with much use of melisma (southern Italy had for centuries been under Spanish rule and Sicily had been under Arab rule too). North Italian folk music was closer to that of Northern Europe: songs were often choral, used triadic harmony and strict rhythm, and were sung in a deep, open voice. They were also more often in narrative or dialogue form; one of the best-known songs, variants of which were found in different parts of the north, was 'Donna lombarda', a grim dialogue not unlike the Scottish ballad 'Edward, Edward' – in it a faithless wife is compelled (as we gradually learn) to swallow the poison she had prepared for her husband.

A special case are the Venetian gondoliers' songs based on whole sections of the Renaissance epics of Ariosto and especially Tasso. According to Romantic authors, some gondoliers knew by heart the whole of Tasso's *Jerusalem Delivered* (20 cantos of some 80, 100, or more eight-line stanzas apiece), but Goethe, when in Venice in 1786, found only two gondoliers able to sing a section; 30 years later, when the practice was on the wane, Byron's friend John Cam Hobhouse knew of a Venetian who could sing some 300 stanzas. The tunes – several were recorded – were genuine folk melodies; they may have been of South Slav origin. The gondoliers' preferred method was to sing alternate stanzas or half-stanzas at a distance from one another (for example when ferrying passengers in opposite directions), each with a good deal of ornamentation. According to Goethe, it sounded best if you stood far away.

Narrative song, however, could also be found in the south; a rare 1780 collection of Sicilian songs includes a spirited dialogue between a young woman and her confessor, who accuses her of making eyes at young men ('a plague take you!' she concludes, 'What a lot of questions!').

Conditions of performance may account for some of these differences. Northern peasants often lived in *cascine*, large farms where great numbers of labourers and their families would get together on winter evenings, sitting in the stable or cowshed for warmth (firewood was scarce and dear). Rice cultivation in the northern plain called for gangs of women who sang work songs or, late in the century, defiant trade union songs. Many southerners lived in large hilltop villages but went out to work on fragmented individual holdings. The characteristic music of such villages – still to be heard in 1950 in southern Tuscany and southwards from there – was the braying of donkeys at about 3 a.m. in summer as each peasant set out for his plot, several miles distant; he himself might sing something more melodious on the way. In Sicily, the great folk singers were long-distance carters who spent the night in a sort of *caravanserai* (a large inn enclosing a courtyard) and held ritual contests, with much capping of improvised virtuoso ornamentation.

Instrumental folk music was, as usual, largely meant for dancing. Stendhal's novel *The Charterhouse of Parma* describes the invading French soldiers of 1796 learning some of the many regional dances from north Italian girls; these dances have since largely disappeared or been commercialized. Home-made fiddles were used for them, as well as tambourines, recorders and pan-pipes made out of bamboo, guitars in the Spanish-influenced south, and different kinds of shawms (medieval oboes) and bagpipes. The barrel organ and the accordion came later in the century. In southern Sardinia an extraordinary triple clarinet was (and still is) played by one man who kept all three pipes (drone, medium, high) going at once by controlled breathing into each in turn; it was used to perform a complicated local form ('mutu' or 'mutettu') developed by strict rules from two opening melodic lines.

Even poor peasants did not always stick to their village. It was, in fact, the poorest hill dwellers who relied on seasonal migration to survive, and some of them migrated as musicians. In Victorian England the Italian barrel-organ player – often a mere boy – was a well-known figure, as were other Italian migrant traders.

Within Italy the most familiar of these seasonal migrants – a few are still to be heard today – were the *zampognari* or bagpipe players. Shortly before Christmas they came down from the hills, to Rome and Naples in particular, and were paid by town families, sometimes year after year, to play and sing before a favourite image of the Virgin or the Christ Child; the custom in Naples, where preparations for Christmas have long been a thriving concern, was to give them a cake as well as money. These bagpipes – less shrill and more guttural than Scottish ones – were sometimes accompanied by a shawm (*piffero*) or a rustic trumpet. There was also a north Italian bagpipe called the *piva*.

What the *zampognari* played seem to have been genuine folk tunes. But country musicians who spent rather more than the Advent season in town inevitably picked up art music, and that, in Italy, meant operatic melodies. A southern hill town, Viggiano, specialized in harpists in the same way as some

Chinese or indeed Italian towns still specialize in turning out restaurant cooks. In the 1850s, when Viggiano numbered some 7,000 inhabitants, about 300 of them were said, at any one time, to be travelling on foot all over Italy and Provence; a few had gone farther still, one or two to the Americas, and had come back after many years with modest fortunes apparently earned by teaching music. These *Viggianesi* played a mixture of folk, religious and operatic tunes. They had been at it for some time: an elderly harpist in the 1850s recalled his grandfather playing arias by the eighteenth-century composers Jommelli and Cimarosa. When in Naples, they also bought Neapolitan songs from street sellers; this suggests that they were involved in the creeping commercialization of the so-called Neapolitan folk song, something that will be dealt with in a later chapter.

In Naples they were competing with native street musicians, such as the *guagliune* (street urchins) who sang operatic tunes to a whistling accompaniment, or else serenaded in bands using such instruments as Jew's-harps, pan-pipes, a sort of marimba, and saucepans covered with skin with a pipe going through the skin. There were, besides, an array of *cantastorie* (storytellers who paraphrased Ariosto and Tasso in Neapolitan dialect, sometimes with a violin accompaniment) and beggars whose dramatic songs could be long and elaborate. Much the same went on in other towns, though with less notice taken of it than in Naples (by definition *the* picturesque Mediterranean city) and maybe with less panache.

In towns, folk music was always likely to be irretrievably mixed with art music. By the early twentieth century this seems to have been true in at least the more accessible parts of the countryside as well, to judge from the researches which the pioneer ethnomusicologist Francesco Balilla Pratella carried out in his native Romagna. He found singer-improvisers at harvest feasts capping each other's verses (with a knife fight sometimes the result) and wandering musicians who played a mixture of dance and operatic tunes in wineshops and at country fairs. At one Easter Monday feast, barrel organ and clarinet carried the melody while a cello accompanied with arpeggio chords or pizzicato. Some of these musicians had been trained by a well-known blind teacher, himself a composer of sacred music.

The striking fact is how folk music was ignored by Italian professional musicians through almost the whole of the nineteenth century, even though the country was experiencing a nationalist movement with which at least one leading composer, Verdi, was in sympathy. Verdi liked to secure examples of music typical of the places where his operas were to be set (which he then failed to use in his scores); he, Donizetti, and others composed songs that used occasional modulations or ornaments characteristic of one or other kind of Italian folk music, but that was as far as it went.

Even the great nationalist leader Giuseppe Mazzini, who in an 1836 essay called for a 'progressive' regeneration of Italian music, had nothing to say about folk music. He shared the usual romantic nationalist belief that music, like language, expressed the unique original genius of the people; he wished Italian music to reflect the historical and local character of its subject matter; he criticized the music of the immediately preceding generation (that is, of Rossini and his followers) as the 'plaything of an imperceptible minority', accomplished but shallow, lacking in thought, religious sense and mystery. Yet, when he looked for a 'solemn and complete representation of the popular element', all he meant was that opera composers should give the chorus more prominence. What most Italians actually sang and played was clearly, for Mazzini, irrelevant; as a townsman and then an exile he may indeed have been scarcely aware of it.

The one notable figure who did take an interest in folk music before the late nineteenth century was the visiting Frenchman Berlioz. Unlike Mazzini or Donizetti or Verdi, he liked to scramble over the rugged hill-country east of Rome; there he made friends with a young local man, Crispino, who liked to think of himself as a bandit. Crispino's welcoming call, notated in Berlioz's memoirs, with its *coup de glotte* or click in the throat in mid-vowel, sounds not unlike some street calls that could still be heard in Rome 20 or 30 years ago. Berlioz describes his enjoyment of another young man's serenade to his girlfriend: 'four or five notes in a falling progression, ending in a long upward wail from the leading note to the tonic', the whole repeated and accompanied by the young man's friends (without regard to harmony) on mandolin, shawm and triangle. Berlioz's experiences crystallized into the 'serenade of a mountaineer in the Abruzzi to his sweetheart' in the third movement of *Harold in Italy*, not a literal transcription, but far more suggestive of a folk tune played on the shawm than anything by an Italian composer.

Why this difference? Italian nationalism, even at its most romantic, with Mazzini, was essentially political. It set out to free the country from outside domination and to unify it; for some it meant achieving popular sovereignty and democracy. But there was no need to go looking for the roots of Italianness, as some in northern Europe went looking for the roots of their national culture. Everybody knew (or thought they knew) where Italy was and who were the Italians. Music was held to be their preserve: among them – Mazzini wrote – it had its 'homeland'. But he meant the art-music that had conquered Europe, that of 'Porpora and Pergolesi' (hallowed names from the early eighteenth century, little of whose actual music he can have heard). To *Risorgimento* nationalists, folk music was almost literally something they did not hear; at most it made a picturesque incident of town life when the pipes came down from the hills.

Professional musicians, then, were unlikely to be gifted peasants. Mazzini was, in a sense, right in his sweeping references to 'Porpora and Pergolesi'. Italy's tradition of art-music was strong and active. It went back several centuries and was continuously evolving. Much the same could be said of the musical profession, which at the beginning of the nineteenth century was still largely regarded as a trade or craft, rather than a high-minded artistic pursuit. Like many trades in a pre-industrial country such as Italy, it ran in families.

Rossini was the son of a trumpeter and a singer; Bellini's father and grandfather were composer-organists. The leader-conductor of the famous Naples San Carlo orchestra, Giuseppe Festa, was the brother of the leading soprano Francesca Festa-Maffei, who in turn was married to a theatrical agent. There were the Mombelli (father and two daughters, all leading singers; mother a member of the Viganò family of leading dancers and choreographers); the Boccabadati-Gazzuoli (mother a leading soprano, father an impresario; four children, all singers, one of them an impresario, another married to the famous baritone Felice Varesi and mother of yet another singer); the Pacini (a singer, a composer, and a music publisher over three generations); the Brambilla (three sisters, all singers, later joined by a niece who married the composer Ponchielli); the Marchisio (two more singing sisters, granddaughters of a violinist, daughters of a piano dealer and an amateur singer, sisters of a pianist and a composer); and many more. Even at the end of the century, when opportunities for a more impersonal kind of musical training had grown, Puccini sprang from four generations of local musicians, and the publishers he dealt with represented the third and fourth generations of the family that had founded the Ricordi firm in 1808. In this the profession followed on from earlier times when the Scarlatti, for instance, included composers (famous and less famous), singers, a violinist, and an impresario; they intermarried with a similar family, the Uttini, and a woman descended from this union gave birth, in 1813, to Giuseppe Verdi.

Even where a musically gifted child was not born into a family of musicians, the chances were that he or she would be taken up in early youth by a teacher who played an essentially parental role. This did not necessarily mean a gentle relationship. Parents could be harsh, with more social approval than such harshness would meet with today. The teacher might be a family friend: the young Antonio Bazzini, later a famous violinist, was the child of an impoverished 'good' family of Brescia; the influential figure, in this case, was his godfather, who was a friend of the leader of the Brescia theatre orchestra, and had him taught. Or else a local maestro might take pupils, often from the immediate neighbourhood, like the then well-known composer J. S. Mayr at Bergamo, who taught the young Donizetti. Some of the best teachers in the early years of the century were said to be the last of the famous castrati, who were, as a rule, highly trained musicians and could teach theory and keyboard playing as well as singing.

A traditional arrangement was for pupils to lodge with the teacher. It was perhaps on the wane from about 1820 though examples can still be found throughout the century. Another long-standing practice was for the children of poor families to be apprenticed to a teacher who taught (and perhaps lodged, fed and clothed) them in exchange for a share in the pupil's future earnings. In the seventeenth and eighteenth centuries some children were, in effect, sold to professionals who speculated on their future earning capacity and who sometimes ended by adopting them. Such arrangements seem to have been confined to potential singers and dancers. There was doubtless little point in speculating on the future earnings, generally modest, of instrumental musicians: until very late in the century, highly-paid virtuoso players such as Paganini were far fewer than successful singers.

Apprenticeships of this kind, at least for singers, and tenors in particular, went on until the Second World War. Among the best known is Caruso's 1891 contract with his singing teacher, by which he was to hand over a quarter of his earnings during the first five years of his professional career. This was a normal, even traditional arrangement for a poor pupil to enter into in exchange for free lessons, as was Caruso's buying himself out of it after his initial success.

Even women might enter into – or, more precisely, be made to enter into – arrangements of this kind. In the conditions of pre-industrial Italy, it has been said, they had a hard time getting a musical training unless they had been born into the profession, because any relationship with a man not a relative was thought compromising. There is some truth in this, but there is also evidence that women could be taught in the family home by visiting teachers, some of whom specialized in this line of work, and as state music schools established themselves many women attended them (still carefully segregated). The real trouble was the assumption that women could not be professional musicians except as singers, keyboard players, or harpists. Even here there were occasional exceptions (like the Ferni sisters, celebrated violinists), but women orchestral players were unthinkable. A glaring example of apprenticeship for a woman is the contract by which the illiterate parents of a 22-year-old budding soprano, Luigia Bendazzi, handed her over in 1850 to the Bologna composer-teacher Federico Dallara. She came to look upon Dallara and his wife as her parents, but the three of them were also involved, for a time, in a murkily neurotic, triangular relationship with sexual overtones. Bendazzi eventually made a considerable career in Verdi roles, created the soprano part in *Simon Boccanegra* and married another minor composer.

The young people who learnt the musician's trade through the filial or near-filial relationship described came, as a rule, of modest families. In a pre-industrial country, work was still generally looked upon as a regrettable necessity; the ideal was to own land, enough of it not to have to do work except perhaps of an unpaid, honorific sort. For women, the shame of appearing on a public stage made musical work still more undesirable, at least according to the conventional outlook. For a musicologist writing early in the century, to be a professional woman musician meant 'prostituting one's breath', 'manoeuvring with one's body', appearing openly 'with painted face and in disguise', exposed to 'the whims of an indiscreet public'. In England, at about the same time, the manager of the King's Theatre in the Haymarket, the home of Italian opera, assumed that 'the only object which can induce a woman of character and education to come on the stage [was] the hope of emolument' – lots of it. Men did not incur quite the same risks, but even towards the end of the century 'good' families resisted letting their sons go in for a musical career; in the 1870s the young baritone Vittorio Carpi, son of a prominent Jewish industrialist, landowner and politician, had to support himself on the pittance he had saved from working in the family firm (though a sympathetic uncle paid for his voice lessons) and then had to change his first name to placate his father.

Some musicians did come of 'good' families, but such families, like that of the violinist Bazzini, had come down in the world, sometimes through the father's business failure and sometimes through political upheaval. A crop of musical vocations came about during and just after the troubled period of French rule from 1796 to 1814, when some families had their lands confiscated, while others lost important posts with sudden changes in the regime, or suffered through high inflation followed by a slump. The great soprano Giuditta Pasta would probably not have gone on the stage but for reasons of this kind; in her finest seasons in Paris she was partnered by another singer whose family had fallen on hard times, the contralto Adelaide Schiassetti, daughter of a Napoleonic general. Later revolutions accounted for the professional careers of Mario (the great tenor, famous in London and Paris who was born a minor noble) and more obscure political exiles who tried to support themselves as musicians or music teachers.

Musicians' letters through most of the century generally show modest levels of education, although on occasion spelling and syntax improve after years of success, betokening an effort at self-improvement. Their manners could be coarse. They swore freely, some women included. To judge from the sanitary regulations of 1798 at La Scala, orchestral players, unless watched, were not particular about where in the theatre they relieved themselves. After an 1838 concert in Rome at which Signora Marzi sang, the visiting British statesman, Gladstone, noted 'We are not accustomed to see ladies spit on the floor in the middle of their songs.'

At the same time the surviving correspondence of people in the professional musical world – which on the whole was a theatrical world too – gives a strong sense of freemasonry. Their tone when writing to people in authority is often deferential, anxious to establish their own respectability; to each other, down to earth, often ribald.

In all this there was some change late in the century, though even then the cult of the loud tenor meant, according to Bernard Shaw (writing in 1892),

picking up any Italian porter, or trooper, or gondolier, or ice-barrow costermonger who can shout a high C; thrusting him into heroic roles; and sending him roaring round the world to pass in every capital over the prostrate body of lyric drama like a steam roller with a powerful whistle . . .

33

In Milan, Turin or Rome the standard of the musicians' manners and education had improved, at any rate in leading theatres and concert halls, but little had changed in a minor industrial town such as Voghera, in Piedmont: a prima donna, on being hissed by the audience at the local theatre, turned her back and, by way of rejoinder, gave both her buttocks a vigorous slap, calling out in dialect 'What a lot of scoundrels!'; a riot ensued and, eventually, an apology from the singer. (It was in this same place in 1893 that, the lights having momentarily been turned off – darkened theatres were not yet the rule – 'a shower descended from the gallery onto the stalls that was not made up of water properly so called'.)

Even as late as the 1930s, after decades when training in state music schools had been the norm, some well-known musicians' letters still contained howlers; one referred to *L'Ohengrin*, along the lines of *L'Orfeo* and *L'Ormindo*. To this day the run of Italian musicians keep something of a craftsmanlike aspect, and are not necessarily well-educated ladies and gentlemen – one reason why the conductor Simon Rattle, as he explained in a 1989 interview, does not wish to conduct Italian opera even though he greatly admires a work like *Simon Boccanegra*: 'one does actually want to hear it sung by the kind of people one wouldn't want to have dinner with!'

This is not to say that in the nineteenth century there were no children of the nobility and the professional classes willing and able to learn music. On the contrary, there were many amateur musicians and they often performed in private houses or in theatres. But in the first half of the century at least they were strictly segregated from professionals. The only exceptions seem to have been noble amateurs who sang sacred music, like the mezzo and bass soloists in the first Italian performance of Rossini's *Stabat Mater*; the bass, a member of an exalted Milan princely family, had earlier taken part in a *Creation* that gave the young Verdi one of his first jobs as a répétiteur. Later in the century the distinction between amateur and professional became rather more blurred, at least in minor towns where resources for full professional performances were often short.

This was, in part, a reversion to old practices: rather than being amateurs in the strict sense of the word, some young musicians were, in effect, unpaid assistants or contributors to performances, waiting their turn for a paid professional post. It was an aspect of the old apprenticeship system, and was a particular characteristic of the old court orchestras and of the municipal ones which multiplied in the course of the century. A young man studying the violin would play for free alongside his teacher (possibly his father or other semi-paternal figure), who himself had a limited engagement and hoped one day to take over one of the established lifelong posts.

Often, principal and unpaid assistant had a formally separate relationship as teacher and pupil in a local music school. But the Italian tradition of music teaching was of individual, face-to-face relationships; all music teaching tends that way and in Italy intensely so. It therefore made less difference than historians often think whether an aspiring musician was a pupil of a state, or church teaching institution, or studied privately. The same teacher often took private as well as institutional pupils and until part-way through the century he did not necessarily draw a clear distinction; in Naples, a government inspector in 1913 found the teachers at the state music school, the Conservatorio, still granting exemption from fees on arbitrary, 'patriarchal' criteria rather than according to the regulations.

Until almost the end of the eighteenth century Italy had had a notable array of music schools, nearly all connected in one way or another with the church. The most famous, the girls' music schools in Venice and the boys' schools in Naples, had been founded as orphanages and, in theory, still were; the word *conservatorio*, more familiar to English-speaking readers in its French form *conservatoire*, originally meant 'refuge'. Other schools, less well known but almost as important, were attached to the seminaries of monastic orders or to the choirs of cathedrals and pilgrimage churches, and there was music teaching in the still less well-documented schools maintained by certain teaching orders. A long-standing practice in some of these schools was to earn money by hiring out the pupils to perform at religious functions; there was also a standing temptation to take paying pupils, and to take castrated boys on favourable terms because this Italian speciality was still thought essential to church choirs, from which women were excluded. But splendid though this teaching tradition was, it decayed rapidly in the late eighteenth century, mainly because of the decline of the monastic orders (hastened, but not caused, by the dissolution of many of them) and perhaps also through economic causes such as inflation.

By the early 1800s most of these schools had disappeared, with a few exceptions like the school attached to the great pilgrimage church at Loreto, which carried on throughout the rest of the century. The response of the Napoleonic governments was to found new state or municipal music schools (or adapt remaining institutions) on the model of the recently founded Paris Conservatoire. These schools did not become central to the shaping of the musical profession until the latter part of the century, and will be studied in a later chapter. In their earlier years they were not so very unlike what had gone before. The well-known Bologna teacher Lorenzo Gibelli, for instance, early in his long life (1719–1812) had been horse trainer to a great Bolognese nobleman, Count Pepoli, who provided him with an education; the musical part of it was entrusted to the great musicologist Padre G. B. Martini, a Franciscan monk. Gibelli lived in a flat in the Pepoli palace through three generations of his patron's family; in extreme old age he crowned his career by teaching the young Rossini in the municipal school newly founded by the Napoleonic regime. He thus bridged the worlds of private aristocratic patronage and would-be impersonal public institutions.

Once reasonably trained, the aspiring professional was ready to seek an engagement. This often happened when he or she was no older than 17 or 18. Allegations – common in the musical world – that in the good old days musicians went through a long grind before daring to perform in public should be taken with a fair helping of salt. In the early nineteenth century life-expectancy was half what it is today; few young musicians or their families could afford to wait to start earning. The training of the great soprano Giuditta Pasta was surprisingly brief and to all appearances casual: début at 18 after a brief period of lessons from three teachers (one of them her uncle, an amateur cellist);

about a year's professional work, with tentative and varying results; another period of study, clearly beneficial, occasioned by pregnancy and lasting no more than a few months; then a great career. Antonio Bazzini is said to have first picked up a violin at seven years of age and been able to give good concert performances at 11. Nor was there a clear correlation between length of training and length of performing life.

Unless a young instrumental musician was apprenticed, formally or not, to a member of a permanent orchestra, getting a series of engagements probably meant extensive travel; for singers this was a virtual certainty now that singing establishments in both court and church were greatly reduced, while the network of opera seasons both in Italy and elsewhere was expanding. Italian musicians were remarkably willing to travel long distances in a country with mostly poor roads and few railways before the 1860s, and where travel by sea (often the best resource along the west coast, all the way from Genoa to Palermo) was still subject to contrary winds; the poorer ones might go on foot. As late as 1872 the London-based conductor Sir Michael Costa, used to the comforts of mid-Victorian travel in Britain, raged at having had to make his way from Naples to the nearest railhead through a crowd of 'sailors, porters, *customs men*, coachmen, boys, beggars, enough to drive one mad, a curse on them all ...'

For a special religious function at Osimo in 1754, in the Marches of eastern Italy, most of the singers and players were drawn from the immediate region, within a radius of 40 miles (60 kilometres) or so, but the organizers looked for solo singers and a leader at Faenza – some 70 miles (110 km) away – or as far afield as Lucca, Rome and Brescia: Turin, however, was thought too far to go. Some eight decades later, at Senigallia, in the same region, the orchestra for the opera season at the important trade fair was recruited from a radius of some 60 to 90 miles (100 to 150 kilometres); a few musicians who refused the wages on offer took engagements still farther from their homes, even at Cadiz in southern Spain. These dealings may give an undue impression of mobility because they took place in the slack season, when many musicians were at a loose end. But there is no doubt that, at least from the 1840s, numerous musicians from Bologna – among them some on the establishment of the municipal orchestra – were willing to travel to Athens and Constantinople to play in the opera season there. Chorus singers also moved readily; at the Senigallia fair in 1833, when the small town was packed out, eight or ten women – probably chorus singers – piled into one room, with a small child for good measure. Just how international these movements might be comes out in a letter sent from Odessa in 1853 to an agent in Paris: a trumpeter and a chorus singer, both Italians and both said to be excellent, were interested in an engagement for the coming season at Rio de Janeiro.

Whether in Odessa, Rio, or at home in Italy, musicians who wished to make a career generally had to negotiate for their engagements with an impresario, often through a professional agent. Even before the coming of the French in 1796 the market had been taking over from old forms of dependence on patrons, whether noble or ecclesiastical. The impresario still served the local hierarchies who controlled the theatres and patronized the municipal orchestras, but the old system of direct management by nobles no longer seemed appropriate, if only because it invariably drove up costs.

In present-day musical life an impresario or agent can be a high-powered figure operating on an international scale, but in nineteenth-century Italy such people were, as a rule, intermediaries or fixers of a homespun kind. Many had themselves been musicians (some of them failed) or else choreographers: putting on the elaborate narrative ballets of the time was good training for theatrical generalship. Some were tradesmen connected with the theatre, such as costume-hirers or printers; at the beginning of the century some of the most notable ones were gambling promoters who had taken advantage of wartime conditions before gambling was banned, among them the flamboyant, near-illiterate, but musically sensitive Domenico Barbaja, who ran the great San Carlo theatre in Naples for over 30 years with short gaps, also for a time ran La Scala and the Vienna opera, and put on Rossini's most ambitious Italian works.

There still remained some scope for career-minded musicians

to find an influential patron. This was probably easiest for singers and especially for women. If they were attractive they could have their careers helped along by one of the noble supervisors of the opera house, or, like the young soprano Felicita Forconi in the 1830s, form a relationship with a rich expatriate Englishman (Rowland Standish) who launched her by putting on performances in his house in Florence. On the other hand, Forconi was a good singer who presently made a success in ordinary theatres: nothing in Italy of the early nineteenth century matched the Parisian traffic in pretty women in and on the fringes of musical theatre. For one thing, Italian audiences were too music-mad and especially too voice-mad to put up with untalented artists for the sake of their looks. For another, the greater earnestness of nineteenth-century life had had some effect on the upper classes. It was in comic opera that the least respectable women-musicians had flourished – and comic opera was under a virtual ban from the 1820s. By 1848 a Naples journal asserted that unmarried women-singers wished only to get married, and married ones to remain faithful to their husbands.

This too perhaps needs to be taken as an impressionistic rather than a scientific statement; but it marked a trend. What can be said is that for much of the nineteenth century the musical profession remained largely insulated from the rest of society, a traditional craft, most of whose members liked to work, eat, talk, joke, quarrel and make love with each other far more than with anybody else.

3 Faded Traditions

To most of us, Italian music in the nineteenth century means opera. We imagine a whole nation intent on that, forgetful of the old sacred music, hardly aware of the new symphonic music and not much enjoying what little did come its way, rescued only towards the end of the century by Arturo Toscanini and one or two other leading conductors. This impression is not totally wrong; it matches the outlook of most nineteenth-century audiences in Italy, for whom, indeed, not much existed outside opera (in other European countries too, opera took up far more of educated people's musical life than it does today). Yet a great deal else was going on, even if not many noticed and fewer remembered.

For much of the eighteenth century, Italy had been central to the making of both sacred and instrumental music: both were part of the role ascribed to it as, by definition, the land of music. The nineteenth-century sequel, faded and straggling as much of it was, is only beginning to be explored.

In 1784 a frail but bright-eyed monk died in Bologna who had never set foot inside an opera house yet knew a great deal about contemporary opera as about every other kind of Western music, old and new. This was Padre Giovanni Battista Martini, the greatest musicologist of his age, who had befriended the young Mozart and corresponded with musicians all over Europe while hardly stirring from his Franciscan convent. In a long lifetime – he was 76 when he died – Martini accumulated a vast collection of music and an equally vast archive of letters. These have come down to us more or less intact and give an extraordinarily detailed picture of musical Italy in the eighteenth century, unmatched by documentation of the nineteenth save perhaps for Verdi's archive, which is only just starting to become fully available. Because Padre Martini was a monk, a great scholar and an expert on counterpoint the people who wrote to him dwelt a good deal on church music; they looked out old manuscripts for him and submitted fugues for his judgment. But because he was a teacher and a friendly, humane person he also heard from young opera singers about the first steps in their careers, was treated as an unpaid agent for professional musicians and heard plenty of gossip, some of it ribald.

A cross-section of around 1750 of this dialogue between Padre Martini and the Italian musical world would show many clusters of musicians in small towns, generally grouped round a church choir. The *maestro di cappella* – 'master of the chapel' (significant term) – was the local composer; he might be a cleric or a layman, but his primary task was to train the choir and its supporting instrumentalists and supply them with music for liturgical purposes. Some of these pieces were routine, psalms and graduals and offertories, others were to mark some exceptional circumstance – a Te Deum giving thanks for a ruler's recovery from illness or cantatas for a saint's festival. After a time the composer piled up a stock of such pieces, which might now and again be recycled – by himself or his successors – though after 30 years or so it was only highly exceptional works that survived, like the famous *Miserere* by Allegri, which the Sistine Chapel choir in Rome guarded as their monopoly. The hilltop towns of central Italy, places like Gubbio, Camerino and Spello, made up a dense network of such small-scale musical centres.

Larger towns had several church or monastic choirs, each a source of new music and work for musicians, who might also be busy with cantatas and other entertainment for the local magnates. In a few great pilgrimage churches (Loreto, Assisi, Padua) the choir was famed as a centre of teaching as well as of new music; even more celebrated were the four charitable girls' orphanages at Venice, with their vocal and instrumental concerts of music by their teachers (Vivaldi and Galuppi among others) and the four equivalent boys' institutions at Naples. In capital cities and in some other towns there was a musicians' association often called the *Accademia* (or *Società*) *Filarmonica*. Its purpose was partly to uphold musicians' status and partly to maintain solidarity and fellowship, so that it had something of the guild or trade union about it; the Bologna academy, the best-known one, set great store by its entrance examinations, and it took a friendly nudge from Padre Martini to get the 14-year-old Mozart through. Members of such 'philharmonic academies' sometimes gave concerts; at Modena the name was borne by the ruling duke's orchestra. But all these diverse institutions masked a fundamental unity. The same people, by and large, sang or played in church, taught – whether privately or in institutions – and, when occasion offered, turned up as *accademici filarmonici*.

Little of this will be new to anyone who knows something of the slightly earlier career of J. S. Bach with his 199 church cantatas, allowing for the distinctiveness of his Lutheran background. Where Italian musicians of 1750 differed from German was in being able to work far more readily in opera.

In the unprecedented half-century of peace Italy enjoyed from 1748, opera seasons multiplied. An ambitious young singer or composer could now begin to think of making a lucrative career in opera alone, although it was prudent to keep, if possible, a place in a church choir as insurance against falling out of fashion or against old age, with some arrangement for leave in the meantime. Even modest singers or players could hope to work in opera during the carnival season at least: singers in the Loreto choir were again and again granted leave to appear in opera, as a rule in minor towns within 30 miles or so, though at Padua the *maestro di cappella* of the great pilgrimage church of St Anthony, Padre Francesco Antonio Vallotti – another Franciscan and something of a disciplinarian – sacked the teenager Gaetano Guadagni for playing truant in too many opera seasons. Guadagni, however, valued his place in the choir and managed to get it back 18 years later, after he had enjoyed an international career and created Gluck's *Orfeo*; eventually, in his retirement, he settled down in Padua as a full-time choir member and a leader of the town's musical and intellectual life.

Soon after Guadagni's dismissal another promising young singer did not even bother to join a church choir: as a correspondent reported to Padre Martini in 1752, he had just sung in opera at Turin and Piacenza 'with fair success, so his father has it in mind … to set him to a theatrical career …'. He did in fact do well as a tenor. Opera was gaining at the expense of church music, and would go on doing so for the rest of the eighteenth century and beyond.

The cause was not just that opera was growing more and more popular. Church music was being run down, because the church itself was inwardly running down. Monastic vocations were fewer; so, from the 1740s or earlier, were castrato singers – involuntary monks of a kind, who were still thought indispensable in church music. All this happened before some religious orders were dissolved by 'enlightened' rulers and others by Napoleon. From the 1760s and especially the 1770s Padre Martini's correspondence shows the strain on church choirs. The leading church in Bergamo was reduced to offering a castrato almost unlimited leave to sing in opera, provided he turned up for Holy Week. If a couple of sopranos in the Sistine Chapel caught cold the *Miserere* would be at risk. An agent in Rome who was trying to recruit singers for the Assisi choir reported that only a miracle worked by the Pope could get anyone to come: 'they say that in Rome they can earn twice as much from (religious) musical functions alone, to say nothing of the opera'; besides, life in Assisi was boring, whereas 'in Rome they are used to endless entertainment'. Assisi had not been thought so boring 20 or 30 years earlier. The famous musical orphanages closed – all the Venetian ones, and all but one in Naples. Music in Italy, it seemed, was turning from the sacred to the profane.

Yet this was in part an illusion. So much church-based music-making went on up and down the country that a good deal of it could vanish and yet still leave behind a respectable bulk.

We know remarkably little about sacred music in nineteenth-century Italy. Apart from one or two well-known compositions it has been largely written off. Yet there was a great deal of it, and a great deal has survived. There are, for instance, 985 extant sacred compositions by Niccolò Zingarelli (1752–1837), whose long career was also taken up with opera and with teaching. Some of the 985 are incomplete and others are no doubt duplicates: the slightly older Giovanni Paisiello, as *maestro di cappella* to Napoleon and to one Bourbon and two Napoleonic kings of Naples, confined himself almost entirely – his health was flagging – to recycling his earlier works under new titles; where necessary he changed the name of the king God was called upon to save. All the same, Zingarelli wrote a lot of sacred music: masses, psalms, graduals, offertories, sequences, hymns, litanies; and his successors in his various posts (St Peter's being the most distinguished) were not far behind.

Who composed sacred music? On the whole it was no longer the first composers of the age. Paisiello had been that; as late as 1855 his *Passion* was still in the catalogue of a leading Naples publisher, as were equally isolated works by still earlier eighteenth-century masters – Pergolesi and Jommelli. But among the nineteenth-century composers, Rossini, Bellini and Verdi each wrote only a handful of sacred works, either to please themselves or for a special occasion. Donizetti wrote more (as he did every other sort of music) but even then nothing like as much as composers who had a church post.

Some of these composers belonged to the composers' 'reserve team'. Among Zingarelli's successors at St Peter's were Francesco Basily and Pietro Raimondi, men who, like him, had a reputation at the time for opera too; today it has sunk almost without trace. (Raimondi's ingenuity – he was renowned for masses and oratorios composed in two or even three blocks that could be performed simultaneously or apart – suggests some of the artefacts shown at the London Great Exhibition of 1851, which he outlived by a couple of years.) Carlo Coccia and Saverio Mercadante were examples of prolific opera composers who, after a decade or two, found that they were not as popular or as well rewarded as Rossini or Donizetti, and both successively took up a cathedral post in the gaunt Piedmontese town of Novara; Mercadante's sacred works had a long enough currency in the Roman Catholic church to be appreciated by

James Joyce. Then there were one or two noted scholar-composers, like Padre Stanislao Mattei, who succeeded Padre Martini as the leading musical authority in Bologna, and taught Rossini and Donizetti: a thoroughly respectable if perhaps not inspiring figure.

Many composers of sacred music, however, were far humbler figures. Like their eighteenth-century predecessors but in smaller numbers, they played the organ, tried to keep up a choir from which castratos had now vanished (as they did everywhere by 1830 except in Rome) and went on producing new works for liturgical use. Who, for instance, was G. B. Balloni, *maestro di cappella* in the small town of Recanati in the Marches of eastern Italy? In 1859 – we know from surviving correspondence – he was writing an antiquarian kind of sacred music using modes and cantus firmus. What can it have been like?

According to distinguished foreigners like Berlioz, this piece – and just about every other piece of music to be heard in Italian churches – was dreadful, a copy of the loudest and crudest sort of comic opera finale when it was not a direct quotation from *The Barber of Seville* itself. But the real situation of church music was not quite so simple.

Italians who went through a formal musical training inherited from the eighteenth-century tradition the 'learned', 'ancient', or 'Palestrina' style, inculcated through repeated exercises in fugue and counterpoint. It was thought to be particularly suited to choral passages. Palestrina's connexion is somewhat vague. He was revered as a father figure, thanks to the legend by which his *Missa Papae Marcelli* had saved religious music from being suppressed by the Council of Trent; and he stood at the head of a small hierarchy of composers – Benedetto Marcello and Pergolesi were the other leading figures – that was thought to represent the true inheritance of Italian sacred music.

This again was a product of legend rather than experience. Padre Martini had known a great deal more (and better) but the legend went on being transmitted; in 1871 it still informed Verdi's advice on a syllabus for music colleges. Interest in Palestrina was further stirred by the publication in 1828 of a biography by Giuseppe Baini, one of a line of Vatican-based musicians who, unusually, never worked in opera. Baini's life was vast but defective; Palestrina scholarship, when it got going in the latter half of the century, was German-led. Meanwhile, Palestrina as individual artist-hero loomed larger than ever; a composer like Raimondi used devices drawn from some of his works, and (so far as we can tell) choral sacred music in general followed on from eighteenth-century Italian practice as it was selectively brought to mind, largely innocent of the rediscovery of Bach going on elsewhere in Europe.

Solo or concerted passages were another matter. Here composers wrote in an idiom close to that of the opera house. This was nothing new. In the eighteenth century it had been common form and not just in Italy: modern audiences can hear it in Mozart's enchanting *Et incarnatus* from the C-minor Mass, the musical equivalent of a rococo angel in wind-blown stucco and gilt.

What was new by 1820 or so was a sense that religious experience ought to be solemn, awestruck. This feeling was strongest in northern European countries that had been most deeply affected by the French revolution and the Romantic movement. Revolution showed what eighteenth-century 'triviality' could lead to; Romanticism set a new value on feeling welling up from the depths. The sense of awe was weakest in a highly traditional, unrevolutionized society like Italy. But, even in Italy, foreigners like Berlioz and Spohr were not the only ones to complain. The cardinal vicar entrusted with keeping order in Rome inveighed again and again – in 1824, 1838, 1842 and 1856 – against musical misdeeds in church: there ought to be no excessively noisy instrumental music – certainly no percussion, – no march tunes, no endless repetition or coloratura, no 'over-brilliant' organ sonatas at the elevation, above all no 'lewd and impure theatre melodies'. There should also be no use of conductor's batons and no chattering among the singers. All these were clearly pretty common. A commission headed by the composer Gasparo Spontini (who had made a great career abroad and was now taken up with charitable works) reported in 1839 that 'horrors' were profaning holy places, by which it meant extracts from Rossini's *The Thieving Magpie* and

Donizetti's *Lucrezia Borgia*. Composers who were active in the church themselves weighed in: Zingarelli and Basily denounced the use of operatic or military music, yet in their own sacred works the one went in for extended coloratura, the other for march tunes and hymns in waltz time.

What did all this amount to? The denunciations may have been largely conventional. The way they were repeated at intervals suggests that the habits they condemned were the natural bent of people for whom the musically sacred and profane were still not quite distinct. If Rossinian crescendos and roulades were the idiom of the moment, why not sing and play them in church? 'Impure theatre melodies' were what the other fellow was up to. This helps us to understand the mixture of elements in Rossini's own *Stabat Mater* (completed version, 1841) where some of the choruses are learnedly fugal while the tenor's jaunty *Cuius animam* still has power to disconcert. The real priorities were brought out by an incident at St Peter's itself: on Easter Sunday, 1829, the choir could not get on with the scheduled *Tu es Petrus* 'because of the noise from the military bands.'

In the latter half of the century Italian religious music becomes even harder to study. Scarcely any of it is known, apart from Verdi's unique *Requiem* and his late, idosyncratic *Four Sacred Pieces*. The abortive *Requiem Mass* for Rossini (1869) for which Verdi lined up 12 other composers besides himself, was performed for the first time in 1988; it suggests that by the last third of the century Italian musicians were going off in various directions, some inspired by Liszt, Mendelssohn or Gounod, others by *Rigoletto* or by Rossini himself, the whole uneven but not contemptible.

The Mass was a special occasion. What was happening in more workaday conditions can be gathered from the experience of two young baritones of about 1850 to 1860. Antonio Cotogni, brought up in Rome as an apprentice ceramics worker, came upon singing as a pursuit in a surviving orphanage (with music school attached) where a cousin had a free place. Cotogni sang treble, then, after his voice broke, studied with a member of another surviving institution, the choir of the great basilica of St Mary Major. He eventually got paid for singing solos in leading

Rome churches; at one oratorio performance where he sang alongside the well-known castrato Domenico Mustafà (a member of the Sistine Chapel choir) the audience demanded an encore so frantically that the police were called in. Soon afterwards, Cotogni made his stage debut; he spent the rest of his splendid career in the opera house, much of it in London and St Petersburg.

A more average career, that of Giovanni Marchetti, began with his being trained by a member of one central Italian church choir (at Loreto) and then joining another (at Orvieto Cathedral); for modest fees he sang solo at yet smaller places like Bolsena, and he probably sang in local opera performances before making his début in a leading theatre at Florence, apparently at the advanced age of 37 or 38. He then worked in opera all over Italy and sometimes abroad, but one of his fellow (male) singers warned him to hang on to his church post (while also joshing him about the supposed homosexual tendencies of choirmasters). By his late 60s Marchetti had lost his money; his first wife and their six children had all died; his second wife was estranged; he joined another choir at Assisi where he got only his meals and an occasional small fee. He could no longer sing in opera, though he had some share in arranging minor Assisi opera seasons; he lived in one small room and was cared for by his landlady, a blacksmith's wife. In his eighty-first year he was still there.

We need to imagine many other careers centred, at least part of the time, on church music – those of organists and instrumental players as well as singers. Such music was no doubt in a bad way; it probably touched a low point in the 1880s and 1890s, when the *maestro* of the Milan Cathedral chapel thought his was virtually the only remaining choir in the country; even then he grumbled about the quality of the choirboys he was having to take on. At San Petronio, the leading church at Bologna, with a glorious musical tradition, the *cappella* had its numbers halved between 1886 and 1896 on its way to extinction in 1920. Early in the next century (1903) the Pope decided to start a thorough reform of church music. Yet there was some continuity all the way through: musicians, often humble, carried on a not ignoble tradition. Without that, one can hardly account for something like the 1970s television film of Luciano Pavarotti and his father (also a tenor) singing César Franck's *Panis angelicus* in a Modena church, and singing it very well.

Instrumental music, like sacred music, depended largely on the existence and prosperity of institutions. Nowhere in Italy at the start of the nineteenth century was there a paying public able to support independent concerts of the kind that had made their way in London, Paris, and Vienna.

Some institutions had vanished, like the Venice orphanages with their girls' orchestras for which Vivaldi had written so many concertos. Others were in temporary eclipse, like the Turin court orchestra, which had likewise contained some of the finest players in the country; it never fully recovered from the absorption of Piedmont into revolutionary and Napoleonic France. Not quite by chance, the leading Italian-born composers of instrumental music at the turn of the century were all working abroad: Luigi Cherubini in France (by then in effect a French composer), the cellist Luigi Boccherini in Spain, and the violinist G.B. Viotti in England. Their works circulated abroad far more than they did in Italy.

The Napoleonic regime, on the other hand, brought a craze for military music and led to the setting up of a number of wind bands, even in small towns. This was a lasting innovation. The wind band in its uniforms became a feature of public holidays and local celebrations, as it still is. It also found its way into opera, where it was to account for some of the literally and figuratively brassiest moments in Verdi's early works: the 'rustic music,' for instance, that accompanies King Duncan's entrance in *Macbeth*, a moment some have found intolerable and others sublime in its apparent naivety. An indirect effect of band mania may have been the overbalancing of the ordinary opera orchestra with excessively strong wind in relation to strings. The string sound itself was weakened by the stubborn shortage in Italy of good viola and cello players: 'There are' Rossini complained as he prepared the Bologna performance of his *Stabat Mater* in 1842, 'few cellists in this land of mortadella'; a quarter-century later Verdi was to demand a full complement of violas and cellos, without which a proper ensemble in a complex late work like *Don Carlos* was not to be had.

Meanwhile, the restoration of the old sovereigns in 1814 brought back some of the old court orchestras; there were also municipal orchestras in towns like Bologna, where the nobility subsidized them through their control of local government (and hence indirect taxes on food which bore hardest on the poor).

These orchestras, at least in northern Italy, were all organized in roughly the same way. The leader controlled day to day running, and could possibly hire and fire, though he might have to defer to a noble supervisor. There was an inner group of players with lifelong appointments on a fixed salary scale, a middle ring of temporaries who might play year after year while waiting to step into a permanent member's shoes, and an outermost ring of apprentices who played for little or no reward. In an orchestra run by a public authority there was some kind of retirement scheme, but not, as a rule, financial provision for adequate pensions: instead, a home-made arrangement let the retired player go on drawing half his pay till his death while his substitute drew the other half. Musicians hung on as long as possible; at Ferrara in about 1820 it was found that several players were too old to perform adequately, one of the violinists was mad, and the second clarinet 'has lost all his teeth and therefore cannot play'.

Where orchestras were unsubsidized, musicians had a rougher time – and so did the music they played. Orchestras were formed for a particular occasion and then disbanded; pay was low. This was true in Rome, where the papal government would not subsidize the performing arts before 1829 and only on a small scale after that. Rossini, in 1816, was startled to discover that the barber who shaved him every morning was the first clarinet in his own *Torvaldo e Dorliska*; a decade and half later, Berlioz found a goldsmith and an upholsterer playing in the same Rome opera house on the side. In other cities, minor, unsubsidized opera houses had the same problems. With the multiplication of theatres and seasons, especially from the 1820s, came that of scratch orchestras on cut-throat wages. 'How can I squeeze any more out of these poor devils?' wrote the leader who was recruiting one of these seasonal bands. But squeeze he did.

Opera was the main business of early nineteenth-century Italian orchestras. There were, all the same, occasions for playing straight instrumental music. What was the repertoire?

By 1814 the main works of the Vienna classical school were nearly all written: Haydn, Mozart and Beethoven might have been thought to pose a challenge to Italian musicians accustomed chiefly to the old elegant school of Cimarosa and Paisiello – a challenge they failed to meet. That is how the situation was read by foreign visitors at the time; because the received history of European music has been dominated by the role of German symphonic music, it has gone on being read that way ever since. Italian musicians failed for many years to come to terms with Beethoven's symphonies in particular: clearly they must have been backward and provincial.

Louis Spohr, the German violinist-composer, was irritated in 1816 to find that the Milan audience enjoyed only the 'singing' solos in his concerto and took no notice of his learned tuttis. In Venice, the orchestra he conducted, in what was probably the first Italian performance of Beethoven's *Second Symphony*, would play only at an unremitting forte; merely to get through such a work was matter for congratulation. A country so bereft of proper German symphonic music was obviously a 'Siberia of art'.

Niccolò Paganini, Italian by birth but an international virtuoso based in France, was asked in 1835–6 to reorganize the Parma orchestra; well-acquainted as he was with the recent work of the Paris Conservatoire orchestra, he thought it essential that the Parma musicians should acquire a conductor of the modern type, distinct from the leader and able to weld the players into a unity: only in this way could they perform Beethoven symphonies and other modern orchestral music so as to 'educate people's minds in right feeling'. But his recommendations failed: habit was too entrenched.

Seen from the Italian point of view, it was rather different. Italian critics in the first half of the century never tired of contrasting their own country's 'melodic' tradition with that of

Germany, which they saw as 'harmonic'. German composers were learned, admirably no doubt, but such a show of learning had no place in Italian music (other than sacred). The ideal remained classical simplicity and ease, with a memorable melodic line unobtrusively, though felicitously, accompanied.

Since Italy was, by definition, the land of music, complacency ruled and people felt free to parrot these musical clichés virtually unaltered. Mozart, one critic declared in 1828 after a performance of *Don Giovanni*, was a great man, but you couldn't go out humming the tunes: 'Why did that good Mozart take it into his head to write music so learned [*scientifica*] as to make singers and orchestra break out into a sweat?' Rossini was again and again charged with having adulterated the pure fount of Italian melody by bringing in far too much noisy German harmony; though couched in the usual platitudinous terms, this was not as foolish as it sounds, for Rossini did bring in more noise, as well as more fizz and speed, than his predecessors had dreamt of – it was a main cause of his success with the less aristocratic nineteenth-century public – and he had indeed committed the sin of letting himself be influenced by Haydn and Mozart, whose works he had studied as a boy.

The Viennese school was not totally ignored or rejected. Certain Italian cities were under Habsburg rule from 1814 and hence, to some degree, under Austrian cultural influence: Venice, Florence, but especially Milan, which had already had a generally good experience of Austrian rule under Maria Theresa and Joseph II; such eighteenth-century buildings as survive in modern industrial Milan show its one-time affinity with central Europe. In Florence a number of cultured foreign residents strengthened what was thought of as the local taste for the intellectual and refined: Rowland Standish, whom we saw launching his favourite soprano, also used the theatre in his palazzo for early performances of Viennese music. It was not difficult in such places to revere Haydn, Mozart and Beethoven as supreme models of the musically great and good: 'Sometimes' a critic wrote in Florence in 1840, 'the public applauds Beethoven because not to applaud would look like too wretchedly open an admission of musical idiocy'. It was another matter to perform them and especially to enjoy them.

In fact, orchestral performances of symphonic works were uncommon anywhere in Europe during the early nineteenth century. Apart from an occasional concert (and then only in a few cities), most people could become acquainted with a Beethoven symphony only by playing through a two-piano arrangement. So there is nothing surprising about Italian performances of Viennese symphonies in piano arrangements or in versions adapted for string quintets. Italy, however, was late in coming to symphonic music as well as selective in the pieces it willingly listened to.

In the first half of the century the works that turn up repeatedly are Haydn's *The Creation* (one Milan performance of which the 21-year-old Verdi conducted), Beethoven's *Septet*, his *Wellington's Victory (The Battle of Vitoria)* and *Christ at the Mount of Olives*; in other words, some of the works now considered least central to his creative output. (The *Septet* even turned up in 1844 in an accordion and piano arrangement.) One hears little of the non-operatic Mozart (and the operas, though given here and there, were not much liked). Beethoven's symphonies were occasionally performed – the *Eroica*, it seems, not until 1854, over half a century after its composition.

His and other Viennese music, most of it written or adapted for piano or small chamber ensemble, was, from time to time, offered by Italian publishers; we do not know how much of it was sold or played, but the Naples firm already mentioned put out two catalogue pages' worth of Beethoven sonatas (plus the inevitable *Septet*) as against 11 pages of display pieces by the virtuosos Thalberg and Herz. In Milan, the leader of the La Scala orchestra in the first third of the century, Alessandro Rolla, played Beethoven quartets with his friends for their own enjoyment, and there was a rare public performance of *Op. 127* in 1842, causing one journalist to describe it and its fellows as 'so difficult and complex that most quartet players think them unmanageable'. But there is no real sign that much of this went beyond a small group of connoisseurs.

Italian composers, for their part, had little incentive to write instrumental music, whether for orchestra or chamber ensemble. Rossini's delightful string sonatas and Bellini's pleasing little oboe concerto were schoolboy exercises, and not followed up. Donizetti was only a little older when he wrote most of his 19 string quartets for his teacher J. S. Mayr and his Bergamo friends to perform; they were agreeable rather than searching. Verdi probably read through some of the Viennese classics in score when he was a student in Milan; he kept a lifelong interest in them, but segregated them in a watertight compartment, away from his work as a budding opera composer. By his début in 1839 the opera craze was at its height; in Milan at least, interest in the Viennese school seems to have been on the wane.

What went on in concerts was usually a string of individual virtuoso performances, sometimes solo and sometimes accompanied (by a piano, a small ensemble, or an orchestra) with instrumental and vocal pieces often sharing a programme and much dependence on operatic medleys and variations on favourite arias. In this, again, Italy was no different from most of Europe. The 'tigers' of the keyboard and the bow came and went as they did elsewhere: Paganini, Liszt, Thalberg; and they aroused the same emotions. Italy's own virtuoso violinist, Antonio Bazzini, followed Paganini in cultivating a demonic side to his artistic personality, with a *Round of Elves* to match Paganini's *Witches*; yet another violinist competed with Paganini's feat of playing a whole piece on one string – in this case, the sextet from *Lucia di Lammermoor*. There were home-grown women pianists, and perhaps more child prodigies than elsewhere. A recital on the ophicleide (a bassoon-like instrument, related to the even more obsolete serpent) between the acts of a Donizetti opera strikes us as odd; it happened in Florence in 1837, but it could have happened in other countries.

Where Italian towns of the early nineteenth century differed from London, Paris, Vienna or Leipzig was not so much in the kind of instrumental music performed as in the relative importance people gave it. There was nothing in Italy remotely like the Gewandhaus orchestral concerts in Leipzig with their serious, attentive audiences. Instrumental music was marginal.

Near the start of the century the favourite performing art was ballet. It was given between the acts of operas (an arrangement more customary than the ophicleide display just mentioned) and its late-eighteenth-century vogue was helped by what many by then felt to be the dreariness of serious opera. Elaborate narrative ballets on historical or exotic subjects, some of them calling for over 200 costumes, went on being performed throughout the first two-thirds of the century. Their appeal was to the eye. Their music ranked low in hierarchical terms; it was assigned to second-rate composers and even to a subsidiary leader of the orchestra. But with the craze for Rossini's operas, which swept the country from 1813 – the year of *Tancredi* – there was no doubt of what Italian audiences liked best. As a journalist put it in 1834 (but could have written it at any time between about 1820 and 1848) 'the opera house is what everybody is talking about'.

4 The Sway of Opera

Going to the opera still seems to most British and American people a special occasion. A middle-aged couple, both of them writers, thought I was living high when they heard that I was going to Covent Garden twice in one week. In Italy during the early nineteenth century, four or five times a week was the norm for the educated classes – at any rate while the season was on. Even in what we should think of as small towns the opera house was the place where everybody who was anybody (and a few who aspired to be somebody) met, night after night, to talk, eat, drink, gamble and now and again to listen to the work being performed.

People who have been inside an Italian opera house of the eighteenth or early nineteenth century will have noticed the vast spaces allotted to foyers, stairs and refreshment rooms. It is all most unlike the cramped passages and packed-out bars of Covent Garden and the Coliseum, to say nothing of Sadler's Wells, the New Theatre, Cardiff, or any large American theatre of the pre-Lincoln Center era. This lack of space is only partly due to the fact that British theatres were built as commercial speculations where every square foot had to pay, whereas many Italian houses were subsidized by the municipality or the state. Even from a commercial point of view it paid the builders of early Italian theatres to give the audience lots of room since until 1814 (in Naples until 1820) the foyers were used for gambling. So long as that meant faro or roulette it was a mainstay of the opera budget. But even when games of chance were forbidden, other pastimes like backgammon went on giving members of the audience harmless pleasure. At the end of the carnival season, too, there would be anything up to 12 masked balls held in the theatre, with accompanying banquets – at once a high spot of the social year, an occasion for some (limited) flirting and breaking down of class barriers and, for the management, a source of profit.

What opera meant for the upper classes can be seen in the admission system. You paid to get into the building and, in many theatres, separately to get into the auditorium; for convenience and cheapness, many people bought a seasonal subscription ticket, at least for the first of these purposes. In the stalls, you paid yet again if you wanted a seat with arm rests, which an usher would unlock. Many people were content to stand or to sit on benches; in nearly all theatres – the all-seated San Carlo in Naples being the great exception – there was plenty of standing or promenading room downstairs. Once inside the theatre, you might not bother to go into the auditorium at all; or you might confine yourself to a few social calls on ladies in their boxes. These were, in effect, miniature drawing rooms, where visitors queued up to chat with the hostess one at a time. At La Scala, until the late 1820s, there were even curtains that could be drawn to close the box off from the auditorium, not (as might be imagined in countries where the theatre had stronger connotations of licence) for scandalous purposes, but to make drawing-room intimacy more complete.

The structure of the building was itself an Italian invention. Its purpose was to show off the ruling groups of a petty Italian state. Though copied abroad, it can no longer be seen in Britain in its original form save for one or two miniature houses like the Georgian theatre at Richmond in North Yorkshire, and they are so small as to give only a faint notion.

The auditorium was usually of a horseshoe, bell or rectangular shape; the sides, all the way to the top, were taken up with boxes ranged in anything up to six tiers. The point of this arrangement was to combine well-defined territorial rights with maximum display. A family – at around 1800 it was still most likely to be a noble family – must not only own the space it sat in but be seen to own it; it must be able to see and be seen by its fellows, while itself remaining distinct.

In most Italian theatres, a box could be owned, sold, mortgaged and let independently of the building itself – mainly because selling boxes was a way of raising money to build the theatre in the first place (a device used in Britain for the Royal Albert Hall). In many theatres, ownership of a box carried with it that of a dressing-room across the passage where servants could prepare drinks and meals. The family, which in eighteenth-century parlance included retainers and servants, could therefore spend a long evening at the theatre and have everything it needed, with the bonus of company, gossip, public display and, from time to time, opera and ballet. In winter there was the further advantage of getting away from an immense palazzo largely unheated and unheatable, with nowhere to linger or entertain your friends. As foreign visitors discovered, and some are still discovering, few places can be as penetratingly cold as a high-ceilinged, stone-built room in a 'sunny' country short of energy resources. The theatre, though inadequately heated by wood-burning stoves, at least offered the warmth of other bodies.

One result of these social arrangements, as a French émigré found in the 1790s, was a press of servants all over the corridors and stairs, with a resultant stench. Even in Italy, not a pioneer of modern public hygiene, the authorities did their best from then on to improve lavatories and impose discipline, though as late as 1850 Mrs Gladstone, wife of the future Prime Minister, was driven out of a minor Naples opera house by the stink. It also became less fashionable to go to the opera with a horde of servants: at La Fenice in Venice, opened in 1792, servants were able to follow the show by peering through grilles let into the back walls of their masters' boxes, but when the theatre was rebuilt in 1837 after a fire the grilles were left out.

The tiers of boxes were hierarchically arrayed. The second tier was normally the best and might be expected during the opera season to be occupied in the main by leading nobles. It included the local ruler's outsize box; in a monarchical theatre like the Regio at Turin (attached to the royal palace) King Charles Felix would sit munching breadsticks, thoroughly at home, while in the equivalent theatre at Parma the performance did not start until the ruling duchess (who happened to be Napoleon's separated wife Marie-Louise) chose to turn up. The upper tiers dwindled in prestige as you moved towards the roof; but Italy was a country with many impoverished nobles and some of these could, on occasion, be found in the topmost tier. For this tier to be made into an undivided gallery (even though walled off, with its own separate entrance and stairs) was a token of relative social openness: it happened early in progressive Milan, very late (1878) in an aristocratic theatre like La Fenice and never at the Comunale in Bologna. By and large, boxes in the early nineteenth century meant nobles, flanked with some officials, lawyers and other professional people, though in Trieste and Leghorn many merchants and shipowners sat there and in Milan the developing middle class was a good deal in evidence.

The stalls were for that same middle class (wives and daughters included in some towns), for students, travellers, officers; these last were sometimes allowed to monopolize the front rows, where they would ogle the ballerinas and occasionally stand so as to block everyone else's view. In Rome many abbés sat there, some of them following the libretto with a bit of candle. The gallery, where there was one, was for shopkeepers, artisans, soldiers, servants; not, in practice, for labourers (admission to the La Scala gallery cost a labourer's daily wage) and not for the vast majority of Italians, who were peasants and never came near an opera house.

This visible hierarchy was not static. It varied from one theatre to another and, within the same theatre, from one season to another. There was also a hierarchy of genres; serious opera was thought best suited to the upper classes, a reckoning that had nothing to do with enjoyment and everything to do with display and cost (in the early nineteenth century serious opera merited a higher admission charge than comic opera, and cost a lot more to put on: in leading theatres all the costumes had to be new and the soloists' made exclusively of silk and velvet). After serious opera came 'semi-serious' opera (the smiling-through-tears kind typified by *La Sonnambula*), then comic opera, followed by plays, all the way down to acrobats, hypnotists and performing monkeys. Of the three main seasons (carnival, spring, autumn) the most fashionable was the serious opera season at the leading theatre in the town (carnival at La Scala and in many other theatres, but autumn at the Comunale, Bologna, and a late spring or summer season, timed to coincide with a trade fair, in various other towns); the least fashionable (short of monkeys) was a season of mixed comic opera and plays at a third-rate theatre. Lady Morgan, the Irish novelist, observed this last in 1820 at the 'smoky and time-stricken' Teatro Pace in Rome, filled with shopkeepers and artisans:

The prompter, with his head popped over the stage-lights, talked to the girls in the pit; the violoncello flirted with a handsome trasteverina [a woman from the crowded district across the Tiber] in the boxes; and a lady in the stage-box blew out the lamplighter's candle as often as he attempted to light it, to the infinite amusement of the audience ...

But this kind of audience, made up of grocers' families and the like, could be found at the main theatre, even in the boxes, in the off season; while the upper classes did not mind dropping in occasionally on puppet operas or indeed on performing animals, so long as it did not disturb the routine of meeting their fellows on most nights at the leading opera house.

The performance, then, went on at least as much in the auditorium and the foyers as on stage. One should not assume from this that the audience was uninterested in what was being sung and played; but its relationship with the performers was of a kind that has since vanished from the western world, Italy included. I have experienced something like it in Bengal, at an all-night performance of a Hindu sacred drama with music, on a subject known to all: there was the same buzz of conversation most of the time, the same coming and going (and eating and drinking and sleeping), and, at crucial moments, the same feeling that the audience had become rapt participants.

In Italy this was felt as late as the 1880s by a young aspiring baritone from the United States. He had been used to 'our calm, collected, coldly critical publics and their leaning-back, lapped-in-luxury, "please-amuse-me" sort of manner.' At Genoa he found the usual noisy audience, who chatted through the first scene and the 'familiar ensemble portions', but they listened to the solos, and now and then a 'premonitory hush' heralded a brilliant passage which then gave the musicians and singers 'the straightforward sympathy and the tangible, though subtle, help of the entire audience.' This bears out earlier accounts by foreign visitors between the 1830s and 1860s, one of whom, the famous British baritone Charles Santley, had experience on both sides of the Italian footlights. Audiences listened (when they listened) phrase by phrase and note by note: a tragic moment brought tears, a well-turned phrase 'a murmur of satisfaction, or a short sharp "*bravo*," very encouraging to the performer', but not prolonged enough to interrupt; if a dog barked, however, or if the singer who had just earned a *bravo* uttered a false note, gales of laughter or, worse, whistling (the Italian form of hissing) would break out. If the work or the performers really displeased, 'the audience hissed, screamed, yelled, hooted, and shouted "*basta! basta!*" ["enough! enough!"]', and in Naples at least they strengthened the effect by blowing through seashells and house keys.

An Italian audience, then, was interested in a performance rather as supporters are in a football match. There were good moments and bad moments and it could take a passionate share in both, but – Berlioz and the German composer Otto Nicolai complained – it seemed not to look for an experience of a work of art as a whole; instead – Berlioz wrote – it wished to consume an opera like a plate of macaroni.

Such an audience, in the early years, was little concerned with dramatic illusion. A German singer appearing in Turin in 1788 found that between scenes she was expected to sit in the directors' box, in full costume and make-up and (since theatres were never darkened) in full view of the audience. This particular custom seems to have come to an end shortly afterwards, but a slightly later episode bears witness to a robust acceptance of theatricality. When the prima donna came on during a night scene, the audience at the leading Rome opera house in 1805 wished to see her better; people called out 'lights, lights!'; the stage lamps were raised, but they smoked; the lamplighter came on and trimmed them; later two more men came on with extra candles; all the while the scene went on and no one turned a hair.

One main reason for this behaviour was that an early nineteenth-century Italian audience did not, as we do, experience a work in the theatre only once, or once in a long while. The normal season (of two to three months) consisted of two operas, both of them preferably new or new to the town; each, if successful, would be performed some 20 times. Since a large part of the audience came to nearly every performance, it is not surprising that once they were familiar with the show they talked through part of it, or that they did all they could to hiss an unpleasing work or singer off the stage for good.

In such conditions the highest excitement could come not on the first night of an opera but on the last, when everyone who did not have a box wanted to savour a known but unrepeatable pleasure. A diarist has left us an account of such a last night – that of Donizetti's *Marino Faliero*, performed in Parma in 1838 with two of the finest singers of the time, the soprano Carolina Unger and the baritone Domenico Cosselli. The audience described already had entrance tickets, but – a few locked seats apart – there were at that time no numbered places:

Right after dinner, or without properly dining, people flocked to the theatre ... [before the locked doors] a growing crowd, a growing buzz; shoving, pushing, one step forward, one back. A shriek: what is it? Nothing, they've trodden on his corns. Someone else, pompously: *Make way, gentlemen, I have to get through*; hisses for an answer. A poor devil, pressed on all sides, renders up his dinner: never mind, go and have a coffee. Impatience, anxiety, discomfort at their height. At last the doors are flung open. Heaven help us! A river in spate! Inside! Easy there! Go back! Where did you learn your manners? I'll deal with you later. Go right ahead. A hat falls off, someone's tie slips back to front (shame!); one man loses a shoe, another a coattail. Inside now, without setting foot on the stairs, all dirty, dishevelled, crumpled. Easy there, gentlemen! One at a time! Your ticket! cries the usher. I've lost it. Into the stalls, at once full as a barrel of anchovies ...

Against this we have to set evidence of many nights when attendance was thin. A full house was the exception. There were many reasons for people to stay away: rain, for one – on a pelting night in Florence only foreigners braved Mediterranean downpour; public events in the small world of the opera audience (nearly everyone knew everyone else: the sentence of life imprisonment in the dreaded Spielberg fortress passed on the liberal nobleman Frederico Confalonieri and others emptied the boxes at La Scala because nobody wanted to go out at a time of what was felt to be a common disaster). Economic crises did as much, and so did revolutions and wars if they came too close. But indifference to the work being performed, and the small size of the groups from which the opera-going public was drawn, were the usual explanations.

Italians could nonetheless display a powerful strain of what was called *entusiasmo, furore, fanatismo*. 'The plaudits of an Italian [stalls audience] at an air they like,' Mrs Piozzi (Dr Johnson's former friend) recorded in 1786, 'when one's nerves are weak and the weather very hot, are all but totally unsupportable.'

This enthusiasm, just as much as hissing and shouted abuse, was deeply suspect to all Italian governments – to republican and Napoleonic ones (but for a few months' unaccustomed liberty right after the coming of the French in 1796–7) no less than to the old sovereigns. Because the opera house was the centre of social life, it was of paramount interest to governments concerned with public order. As the (Italian) head of the Austrian government of Lombardy-Venetia put it in 1825, opera at La Scala 'attracts to a place open to observation during the houses of darkness a large part of the educated population'. This was a good thing if it kept young men from discussing subversive ideas in cafés or getting up to immoral conduct elsewhere, but it held its own dangers of scandal and riot.

Hence the strong police and military presence in the theatre. We should visualize an Italian opera performance before 1870 with plenty of uniforms dotted about – not just the off-duty officers goggling in the front rows but other soldiers and police on duty in the auditorium, the foyers, the backstage area and outside the doors. They had their own commanders on the spot, and there was also, sitting in a special box, a member of the supervisory body appointed by the government to control theatres. Any of these officials might order the guard to arrest members of the company or the audience or, in extreme cases, to clear the theatre.

Grounds for arrest were breaches of the regulations. All Italian governments laid down highly detailed rules of conduct in the opera house. There must be no excessive noise, no loud demonstration for or against. Encores (often called for) were generally prohibited, and so were curtain calls save at the end of an act. If the ruler was present, etiquette forbade any applause unless he or she began it – and, on first nights especially, rulers had a trick of withholding applause, to the dismay of composers whose work fell on a seemingly icy silence. Even worse, as the young composer Giovanni Pacini found at the San Carlo, Naples, was silence followed by a pre-emptive shushing – rather like what the Bayreuth audience still gets up to, out of the same misplaced reverence, at *Parsifal*.

What were governments afraid of? Riot was not just a fancied danger. Eighteenth-century audiences had at times been rowdy; they and their nineteenth-century successors often split into factions championing rival prima donnas or ballerinas (as was still happening 30 years ago over Tebaldi and Callas). After the revolutionary period such faction fights might spell political trouble – might indeed be used as an outlet for political sentiments that could not be openly voiced. The papal government therefore put up a flogging block as a warning outside the Rome theatre where a prima donna was winning excessive applause; at Reggio Emilia in 1841 the factions became so violent that the authorities, for a time, expelled one singer's noble partisans from the town; even then the season had to be cut short.

Governments, however, were much more concerned with decorum and with making a show of paternal authority. That was the point of the prohibitions on applause, encores and curtain calls – which could from time to time be graciously relaxed. Even then, audiences sometimes got their own back, like the Naples audience that called out to the king in dialect 'If you don't clap, we will' (they won leave to applaud the tenor Rubini) or the notoriously difficult Parma and Bologna public, whose influence can be seen in the concessions (some encores, some curtain calls) granted in the 1850s.

Censorship, too, was far more a matter of enforcing fussy rules of decorum and avoiding social disturbance than of striking out nationalist or liberal sentiments – at any rate until the Italian governments got a real fright from the 1848 revolutions.

The alleged close bond between early nineteenth-century Italian opera and liberal nationalism is one of those clichés that go marching on in the face of evidence. Governments were indeed on the alert for signs of hankering after even such limited unity as Napoleon had brought to parts of northern Italy: the Parma chief of police in 1837 swooped down on the dress rehearsal of *Lucia di Lammermoor* and threatened to send everyone to gaol because the costumes for the chorus were red, white and green, the Napoleonic tricolour (which no one in the company had had in mind; the designer was probably looking for a tartan effect). But there is no sign that musicians or librettists before the late 1840s were eager to voice nationalist feeling.

Among composers, Rossini and the then famous Pacini upheld the old sovereigns. Bellini and Donizetti seem not to have cared much, if at all; Bellini was cheerfully ready to delete, for Italian consumption, all references to liberty in his *I puritani*, originally written for Paris (*libertà* in the martial duet was simply changed to *lealtà*, 'loyalty'), while the Gaulish rebels in *Norma* were so far from being read in nationalistic vein that the work was successfully performed in 1838 before the visiting Austrian emperor. Donizetti may have entertained some nationalist feeling, but if so it was not strong enough to prevent him from taking (when he was already successful) a post in Vienna as court composer to that same emperor, the supposed oppressor of his country. Verdi, who was a liberal and probably, to begin with, a republican democrat, was able to express, in the chorus of the Jews by the waters of Babylon ('Va pensiero'), a general longing for a fatherland which bothered the Austrian censorship not at all; he dedicated this opera (*Nabucco*) and the next (*I Lombardi*), which had a similar chorus, to two Austrian archduchesses in turn.

What did bother the censorship was, firstly, anything to do with Christian ritual, clergy or saints (*I Lombardi* got into trouble over the baptism scene and the words 'Ave Maria', not over nationalism) or any theme flagrantly opposed to Christian doctrine, like suicide (once heroes and heroines started dying in Italian opera, surprising numbers of them expired on stage without visible cause: Juliet, for instance, managed without a dagger). Furthermore, it did not do for kings to misbehave: the Turin censorship in 1821 threw out a libretto about the Roman emperor Titus and his love for Queen Berenice, presumably because a ruler ought not to be shown having an illicit affair – and then giving it up in deference to popular feeling. Finally, the censors minded dreadfully anything in the slightest risqué or liable to provoke gossip; Cinderella's slipper had to become a bracelet, while her name, Angiolina, must not give Rossini's opera its title, for there was in Rome a well-known young woman so called, and who knew what tittle-tattle that might lead to? As for making fun of a living person, even though only an eccentric poet, that was out; so was showing up the misconduct of living aristocrats' fifteenth-century ancestors – *I due Foscari* was turned down in Venice on those grounds, as an act of self-censorship by the directors of La Fenice, though they relented once another city had taken responsibility for the first performance.

Political censorship was to become a real problem once the full flood of Romanticism with its cult of violence hit Italy, as it did belatedly in the 1840s, and in particular when memories of 1848 made it seem, in the minds of the respectable, all the more dangerous. Hence Verdi's well-known difficulties over regicide in *Rigoletto* (1851) and *Un ballo in maschera* (1859). Even then, a detailed study of how the various censors treated *Rigoletto* has shown that they minded immorality and vulgarity at least as much: Maddalena must not be a tart (a ruling which made the duke's presence in a low dive hard to explain); in Rome and Naples they banned such 'low' words as 'buffoon' and 'sack'. Those cities were always the most obscurantist, Habsburg-ruled Milan and Florence the most reasonable.

In their dull way, the censors who ruled out 'buffoon' and

'sack' were belated followers of a way of thinking that had swayed opera audiences for many years. The cult of the specific – with its promise of the picturesque, the bizarre, the extreme – was a romantic discovery which educated Italians were slow to admit. Their tradition was wholly classical; it valued the general, the elevated and they considered that a work such as an opera should be unified in tone and texture.

True, audiences of about 1800 seem to have been bored with most serious opera which embodied these virtues, and insatiably eager for comic opera, which relaxed into a fair measure of childishness. But it was quite another thing to approve of serious operas that whipped up violent emotions or dwelt on the common or the grotesque. Unhappy endings were thought to make for bad digestion and generally to discompose an audience; this might be a serious matter if the audience included great people. Rossini's *Otello* was at one point fitted with a happy ending (Othello discovered it was all a mistake) and even in 1828, when tragic endings had begun to come in, an opera about Joan of Arc was made to end with Joan's escape from prison and a little allegretto chorus – because it was being performed in Naples as a royal birthday gala.

In this, as in all else, Rossini was the great architect of early nineteenth-century Italian opera. His comic operas were highly successful, but they were almost the last of their kind: peace in 1814 brought a new earnestness as well as a new suspicion of a genre that had allowed much improvised foolery, putting at risk those very proprieties beloved of censors; after *La Cenerentola* (1817) Rossini wrote no more comic operas for Italy. Instead he turned out a line of serious and 'semi-serious' works, culminating in *Semiramide* (1823), that set the mould of Italian opera for a generation.

Rossini did not invent the formal devices that now shaped Italian opera – they had grown up piecemeal at the hands of composers now largely forgotten – but he codified them, and the vogue for his work was such that he made serious opera, once again, what 'everyone' wanted to hear. In the 1820s no composer except Bellini could help imitating Rossini and even Bellini, on occasion, succumbed.

Serious opera now largely displaced comic opera, but it took over many comic-opera devices. Gone was the string of elaborate solo arias which we no longer hear except in Handel's operas or in an occasional revival of Mozart's youthful works; gone too were prolonged stretches of 'dry' recitative (unaccompanied save for the harpsichord). Instead, the aria became an engine for releasing emotion – with a relatively slow or reflective first part giving way to a more rapid second part, often justified dramatically by inserting at that point a sudden twist in the plot, and scored so as to bring, with any luck, torrents of applause at the end. On the model of the comic-opera finale, each act became a continuous structure of such slow-fast movements, many of them duets or larger concerted pieces rather than arias. The whole culminated in a final scene with everyone on stage: a dramatic crisis, a slow, solemn ensemble in which collective emotion was allowed to expand as though time was suspended and finally a rapid discharge of tension in a brief movement called *stretta*; the standard example is the marriage contract scene in *Lucia di Lammermoor*, usually known as the sextet.

This was a classical scheme in that it imposed a set of elaborate formal rules within which emotion, however strong, had to be contained. The composer's task was to provide something new without bursting the frame. It was none too easy; in their football supporters' way, Italian audiences were knowledgeable and fussy; they were apt to complain that Donizetti's many operas held 'reminiscences' of his earlier work, yet when Bellini broke the rules by not ending the first half of *Norma* with the usual ensemble (instead he had a highly dramatic trio with snatches of menacing offstage chorus) that too was initially thought suspect.

The singer's task was to rouse powerful emotions without losing command of vocal writing that still, in the years around 1830, called for some coloratura fireworks and, against spare instrumentation, remained perilously exposed. But it was no accident that the two foremost singers of that time, Giuditta Pasta and Maria Malibran, had technically awkward voices which they schooled with difficulty: tragic grandeur and pathos in Pasta and daemonic intensity in Malibran were what contemporaries remembered, along with uncommon musicianship.

There were many other singers almost as accomplished – some of them technically more secure. Otto Nicolai, though contemptuous of everything else about Italian opera at the time of writing (he had just arrived and his experience was limited to Verona and Rome, not the most musical of towns), raved about singers such as the now forgotten Almerinda Manzocchi in Donizetti's *Anna Bolena*: 'What voices! What skill! What schooling!'

The 1830s were years of intense creativity. This was true in quantitative terms – La Scala launched 38 new operas between 1831 and 1840, more than in any other decade; over Italy as a whole there may have been more new works produced per year in the late eighteenth century, the heyday of comic opera, but many of those had been slight and repetitive, whereas the 1830s saw the mature, committed works of Bellini and Donizetti, as well as those of composers then highly regarded, such as Mercadante.

Towards the end of the decade, as the violent and sombre themes of northern Romantic literature began to penetrate further into Italian opera, so the musical action began to move more rapidly, the orchestral texture thickened and vocal writing became more jagged and required more force. Legend has it that the French (but Italian-trained) Gilbert-Louis Duprez was the first tenor to hit a 'chest-high C', thrillingly vibrant, with a sexual charge which the high notes of tenors using their head voice had not provided; there are, however, signs that tenors had been feeling their way towards this effect for some years before. These changes opened the way for the young Verdi and for the intense energy of a work like *Ernani* (1844), which Shaw was memorably to call 'that ultra-classical product of romanticism, the grandiose Italian opera in which the executive art consists in a splendid display of personal heroics, and the drama arises out of the simplest and most universal stimulants to them.'

Italian critics sometimes grumbled at the new blatancy, but Italian audiences were swept along; the instant success of *Nabucco* (1842), with 57 performances in its first year at La Scala alone, was unprecedented. To people looking back after the hectic period of revolutions and wars of independence, the run-up to 1848 seemed a golden age of Italian opera.

That was when musical (in practice operatic) journals multiplied and were eagerly awaited and read; when the fortunes of the local season took up a large share of polite conversation, and of some impolite conversation as well. In Rome, the great dialect poet, Belli, wrote a string of mordant sonnets commenting almost day by day on the incidents of the opera season; at Naples in 1846 the tunes from Pacini's opera of the previous year were played by military bands in the park, by barrel organs in the main shopping street, by organists in church, even at a funeral, and, although we have no direct evidence, they were probably being sold by hawkers as cheap flysheets. People who could not afford to go to the opera thus still got to hear them – those who had not already hung about the stage door listening for snatches, as some did. For a more affluent or more cultivated audience, publishers brought out many vocal scores, as well as single arias with piano accompaniment or else transcribed for piano, for violin or for cornet, among other instruments.

Some reservations still have to be made. All this musical activity went on in towns – and perhaps only in the 'better' parts of town; the countryside was as yet scarcely affected. Pianos and other musical instruments were almost certainly fewer in Italy than in north European countries (it seems to have been more common to hire than to buy a piano). We have no figures for the sales of vocal scores and transcriptions, but near the end of the century Italian sheet music was still far dearer than British, suggesting a limited market. Musical journals, again with a high subscription charge, circulated chiefly among boxholders and within the musical profession. Against all this, Italian towns had a vigorous street life that made for ready communication – of music as well as news and gossip.

Writing a generation later, in 1869, an author of popular self-help books had *Nabucco* in mind when he wrote that

no one who did not live in Italy before 1848 can imagine what the opera house meant in those days. It was the only outlet for public life, and everyone took part. The success of a new opera was a capital event that stirred to its depths the town lucky enough to have witnessed it, and word of it ran all over Italy.

There was in this some exaggeration. 'Everyone' did not mean everyone. All the same, the writer was talking about a genuine, common passion for opera that, by 1869, was gone. Its departure was masked for a time by the continuing huge success of Verdi, whose three most popular works – *Rigoletto, Il trovatore*, and *La traviata*, performed, hummed, and ground out all over the world – all dated from the immediate post-1848 period. But Verdi's was an increasingly isolated voice. Italian opera had been closely bound up with the world of the old sovereigns. It was shaken when the 1848 revolutions shook their rule; when, in 1859–60, they departed for good, Italian opera began to die.

5 The Musician's Life

In 1833, four new operas by Donizetti had their first performances – in Rome, Florence, Rome again, and Milan. Such a rate of composition was typical of a career that had got under way in 1818: with the last of these 1833 works Donizetti reached his forty-first opera. It was also the rate at which many earlier and some contemporary musicians worked.

The opera composed for Florence, *Parisina* – Donizetti had to write it in a greater hurry than usual because the librettist was late with his work – brought him together, not for the first time, with the impresario Alessandro Lanari. The two of them signed a contract for another opera, which Donizetti would provide for the 1834 carnival season, again in Florence. But in summer 1833 a temporary misunderstanding clouded their dealings; it is worth looking into because it illustrates the strains which the conditions of early nineteenth-century musical life put upon musicians.

We know about it from a long and prolix letter which Donizetti sent to Lanari. Lanari, it seems, had referred to him as a child, and Donizetti began with an – in truth – rather adolescent-sounding refutation of this, with a mock-pompous parade of learning to show that it takes two to make an agreement. He went on:

I asked you to begin with to put on my opera next carnival a little earlier than we had agreed, if you could do it without inconvenience, because I had other commitments. You with your ready understanding replied: 'very well, I'll leave you free to go elsewhere if you like, and we'll put off our opera to another season; only let me know if you do go elsewhere, so that I can secure another composer.'

This answer was quite out of order when I was only asking to open a few days earlier than we had agreed; but, thinking that perhaps you were not anxious to keep me on, I thought to myself: 'it's best to put up with it and respect his feelings'; but then I thought: 'if he wants to be told whether I do arrange another contract or not, it means beyond doubt that he is not sorry to keep me on. So I am obliged to him, and I'll let him know.' And so I did. But sad to say, the way you're acting now is quite unlike your previous conduct. The moment I told you I could work for you and hadn't made another contract, you answered that, having become aware that I wished to work elsewhere, you had let your business dealings slide, and therefore we should speak no longer of this coming carnival but of the following one. What kind of talk is this?

If you let your business dealings slide, I certainly am not to blame. If that's how it is, why did you write to me in good faith 'let me know if you engage yourself elsewhere, so that I can secure another composer' – showing that your business dealings were going forward as before? And even if I were to accept that you let things slide on my account, why didn't you wait for me to say 'I will,' or 'I won't write the opera for next carnival'? And why did you want to know if I would stick with you when you were letting things slide for lack of my contribution, while later, when I told you I could work for you, you had already given up all negotiations? Why not say 'no' from the start, or propose the following carnival from the start?

The letter went on with more recrimination and self-justification, some of which will be examined later. Meanwhile, the first thing to strike a twentieth-century reader is that nowadays a couple of telephone calls would have cleared up the whole misunderstanding in a few minutes. It does seem to have been a misunderstanding – Lanari's 1834 carnival season took place and Donizetti wrote an opera for it – though Lanari may have engaged in some tactical jockeying for position. The real trouble was that in early nineteenth-century Italy a rapid, almost frantic rhythm of musical production (not unlike that of modern cinema or television) depended on means of communication still worked by horses and sails.

In a country where music was dispersed among many cities and towns, nearly everything had to be arranged by letter; the speed at which the letters (and their authors) travelled had roughly doubled since the mid-seventeenth century, thanks to improved roads, but that still meant six days to go from Rome to Venice and eight from Milan to Naples. If Italians of that period were anything like Italians today, they must have greatly preferred doing business face to face to doing everything impersonally, on paper and at a distance, but they had no choice. Some theatrical agents (who dealt mainly with opera) seem to have written, on average, more than 20 letters a day, including Sundays and holidays. In writing every few days and answering every letter, even if nothing had changed since the last, they behaved like medieval merchants, anxious not to lose the thread of dialogue with correspondents perilously far off. Composers, singers and other musicians wrote fewer letters, but, unless they were content to play out their lives in a modest local setting, they still had to deal with a criss-cross of communications that might easily become a tangle. Donizetti was a competent man of business and a generally cordial person, but this letter shows how he too could work himself into a lather as he sought to keep hold of his various engagements.

Much of the work available to musicians was seasonal; even players in a municipal orchestra such as that of Bologna had slack periods, particularly in the summer, when the upper classes made for their country villas. The better players, as we have seen, might then be able to choose between an engagement at a trade fair in Italy and another, perhaps better-paying, engagement at Cadiz or Athens; even humbler musicians were ready to travel 60 or 90 miles (100 or 150 km) to a seasonal job. So, on occasion, were members of opera choruses.

These, the humblest of musicians of all – or, as they were once grandly called, 'the pariahs of art' – were, most of them, drawn from among seamstresses, hawkers, market stallholders and the like, who sang part-time and could not read music (the reason the directors of La Fenice, Venice, gave for putting *La Traviata* into the costumes of the year 1700 or thereabouts was that in contemporary dress the chorus would never have got away with pretending to be ladies and gentlemen). When choruses travelled it was sometimes as strikebreakers; local strikes over pay and conditions were not unknown, though not often successful except in times of turmoil such as the 1848 revolutions. Another reason for travelling was the spread of Italian opera to places like Havana and Odessa that could not raise their own choruses. In the latter nineteenth century some Italian opera troupes were to fail in places like San Francisco or some steamy port in Brazil: members of the chorus could then be seen reverting to their trade as fruit-sellers and the like to raise the fare home.

In Italy itself, a musician – composer, singer, or player – who was not committed in the first place to the church was likely to be pursuing several sets of negotiations at once. He or she was, with any luck, working in the current season of opera in one town (to miss a season was generally reckoned the worst possible advertisement), perhaps disputing payment for the last season in another town, preparing for the coming season in a third and negotiating contracts for yet more seasons in fourth and fifth towns later on. The current season, meanwhile, was not a matter of running through and performing a series of long familiar works. On the contrary, it generally meant learning and rehearsing new works that – like a modern musical comedy – were sometimes being written and rewritten up to the first performance and even beyond.

Take the characteristic schedule of a carnival season, which normally opened with the first of two new operas on 26 or 27 December. Everyone hoped to be busy in an autumn season (probably in another town), which as a rule would end on 30 November. The company could therefore not be expected to turn up for rehearsals before a date some way into December, often 6 December, though by custom it was all right to turn up by 10 December if no earlier date had been specified in the performer's contract. The composer of the first opera should have received the libretto by late August or early September, and was usually supposed to have the entire score ready by 15 December.

For one reason or another, however, managements might not

decide until mid-October on the operas to be performed, and even without this hazard the libretto was often late. The best Italian librettist, Felice Romani, was also the most dilatory; his *Lucrezia Borgia* (for Donizetti) was not fully ready until 26 November, a revised version of an earlier libretto was still missing Act 2 by 15 November, and so on. Musicians cursed and sometimes, like Bellini, quarrelled with him, but in practice they put up with his exasperating ways for the sake of his clear construction and elegant verse. In the early years of the century Zingarelli is said to have composed a serious opera in two weeks (on a libretto written in 12 days). As orchestration grew more complex, even fast workers like Rossini, Donizetti and Pacini needed three to four weeks. Bellini, an uncommonly self-conscious artist, needed two months (and nearly a year between operas to work up sketches).

For singers and players this timetable meant that they had to be quick studies and work hard. In about 1820 the time needed to learn a leading part in a serious opera was generally reckoned to be 15 days, in a comic opera, 10 days; by the 1860s and 70s the time had stretched a little – to 20 days. But in the early part of the century the company had not only to learn the first opera in a brief run-up to Boxing Day (26 December); they had to learn the second opera, on much the same timetable, while performing the first, and if one of the two operas failed they might have to rush on to the stage – within four days if need be – a 'fall-back opera' which some of them might be familiar with, some not. (Those who did not know the work would have their parts cut or would substitute arias from other operas which they did know – one of the more common uses for the 'suitcase arias' which singers took about with them on their travels.)

Rehearsals for a carnival or spring season might go on in draughty, unheated theatres or in the 'Alpine' cold of an old palazzo – that was where Rossini composed much of *The Barber of Seville* in January 1816 with the company talking and joking (and shivering) around him. For most of the century these conditions remained unchanged. Mrs Norton, a good New England housewife, mother of the aspiring singer who was to become famous as Lillian Nordica, wrote home from Milan in March 1879 that she was taking a hot brick to rehearsals to warm

Lilly's feet between scenes; later, in December, their lodgings at Novara had a 'straw carpet on a stone floor; thermometer 7 degrees below; a fireplace no bigger than a good-sized keeler to wash dishes in', while Lilly herself reported '4 degrees below in the room where I rehearse'. St Petersburg, when she got there not long afterwards, was much more comfortable.

A final hardship, as it seems to us, was that most opera companies had to perform four or five times a week, with not only the same orchestra and chorus but the same soloists – a thing unheard of today. One lot of soloists for the whole season was the norm; only La Scala and the San Carlo could afford two – most of the time. Because opera was developing away from recitative and towards heavier vocal writing and orchestration, singers came to prefer giving three or at most four performances a week, but even established stars might agree to give five, partly to help the management and partly to earn as much money as possible. Some went further. The soprano Giuseppina Strepponi (Verdi's future companion and wife) at one time sang Norma, a particularly taxing part, six times in one week when in the early stages of pregnancy. She miscarried, and within a few years she wrecked her voice. Others, however, knew how far to go. Teresa Brambilla, one of the three singing sisters, declared in 1849 that she would never again sing more than four times a week, and would choose only operas that suited her: 'In the past, I played havoc with my voice for the sake of making a name; now that I have made it, I'd be a fool not to take reasonable advantage of it'. She went on to sing Gilda in the first performance of *Rigoletto*.

The results of working in these conditions were unpredictable. The company might well reach the dress rehearsal in the state described by a contemporary observer in 1825:

... the singers tired and hoarse, the orchestra hesitant, the costumes held together with pins, the paint on the scenery still fresh, the carpenters hammering away, the whole, amid the singers' roulades, forming a Babel and an undigested chaos, destined to reach maturity in the course of the performances!

Sometimes the dress rehearsal ended at 3 a.m. on the morning of the first performance, as happened with Donizetti's *Alina regina di Golconda* (1828). On that occasion the first night was an unexpected roaring success – probably because everyone rallied with a final burst of nervous energy. Other first nights were near-failures because the company was tired out, among them those of works that went on to become perennial hits like *La Cenerentola* and *Norma*.

There were other hazards, again resulting from slow communications superimposed on a tight schedule. The full score of an opera already given in another town might arrive late – two days before the first night – and be found to disagree with the orchestral parts received earlier. Not all companies had understudies; if a leading singer fell ill it might take several days to find a replacement – hence some performances in which hoarse singers did their best, and others in which one singer's part was simply left out. A *Sonnambula* without the tenor hero (as performed in Florence in 1839) must have been an odd experience.

No wonder Italians who succeeded abroad wanted never to work in their own country again – so at least thought Mme Adolphe Nourrit, wife of a famous French tenor who misguidedly tried to work in Italian conditions for which he was quite unprepared. Luigia Boccabadati, a well-known soprano, testified that in a year's engagement at the Naples royal theatres she had sung 26 operas (some of them in one act), and that she had had to learn Donizetti's *Imelda de' Lambertazzi*, a full-length work, in six days. (She was suing the management, which had refused to pay her on the grounds that she had been unable to sing through illness beyond the leeway allowed by her contract. She won her case.) But, rather than a hopeless rat-race, the musicians' experience was of a hard school which the best of them were able to master, and which only on occasion tumbled into catastrophe.

How a leading singer might learn a part in five days was exemplified by the visiting soprano Gertrud Elisabeth Mara. She was late for the Turin carnival season of 1788, very late, for she arrived (having travelled from London day and night) five days before the first performance. It was all her own fault; she had tried to put off her engagement in the hope of getting better offers at home. Mara, however, was a seasoned professional, not just a singer but a trained musician, German by birth but brought up on Italian opera. Through the remaining five days she got up at 6 a.m., drank tea; from 7 a.m. to 9 a.m. she went through her part; from 10 a.m. to 1 p.m. rehearsed at her lodgings (as was the custom) with other members of the company; between 1 p.m. and 4 p.m. (though she does not say so) she presumably had dinner and a rest; from 4 p.m. to 6 p.m. she went through her part, as she did again, after a tea break, from 7 p.m. to 9 p.m.; from 9 p.m. to 11 p.m. she had supper and a rest and from 11 p.m. to 1 a.m. she went through her part yet once more. She learnt it in time for the first performance.

There were yet more extraordinary feats of improvisation and memory. If the nobleman who managed the opera house at Como in the mid 1830s is to be believed, a cast who in the morning 'knew nothing' of *L'elisir d'amore* rehearsed for seven hours and, that evening, gave a tremendously successful performance. (The prompter, all the same, may have had a share in the proceedings.) In 1857, by which time new operas were less common and singers expected to perform an existing, familiar repertoire, the baritone Ferdinando Marimpietri rather unusually had to learn the part of Figaro in *The Barber of Seville* within three days ('to which I added the nights'); the first rehearsal took place on Thursday morning and the first performance (at Bastia in Corsica) on Sunday night.

A fast, well-schooled routine, however, was the distinguishing mark of Italian musicians in the early part of the century, rather than breakneck improvisation. The experienced British manager of the King's Theatre in the Haymarket contrasted, in the 1820s, 'the careful and gradual getting up of the operas' in Italy with the slapdash methods of the London stage.

On the other hand, Italians could scarcely credit the slowness of the Paris Opéra – what Verdi's wife called its 'machinery of marble and lead'. There, elaborate productions ruled; it might take 24 hours to decide whether a singer should raise a finger or the whole hand, and a new opera (running, it is true, for five hours and incorporating two ballets) would be in rehearsal for several months. Verdi's own *The Sicilian Vespers*, written for

Paris on the 'marble and lead' system, was given at Parma in the ensuing carnival season with the usual 20-day rehearsal period. 'It's a miracle that they manage to perform it at all!' Verdi wrote. But perform it they did, opening on Boxing Night as usual.

Much later, a few musicians were to have the opportunity of prolonged study. Rosa Ponselle, the Italo–American soprano, was given two years to prepare her famous 1927 Norma at the Metropolitan; before the 1927 season she and the contralto who was to sing Adalgisa spent a five-week summer holiday rehearsing their duets, on a timetable only a little less exacting than Mara's. This kind of deep digging was out of the question for early nineteenth-century Italians. The original Norma, Guiditta Pasta, had the usual three-week rehearsal period; she reached Boxing Night in a high state of nerves, declaring that if she failed in the part she would give up the stage, and, as we know, it took a performance or two to get everything right. Ponselle was unequalled as Norma in our century as Pasta was in hers; we cannot compare them, but we need not assume that Ponselle's two years made for a finer performance than Pasta's three weeks. (Pasta was working within a living tradition; Ponselle had to reconstitute it.)

The exacting demands of an Italian career, and the way nearly every musician of consequence moved around the same circuit, made for a powerful sense of competition. Much of this was inevitable in an art that depended on the individual's hard-won control of his or her own body. What Lillian Nordica wrote about singers is true of solo instrumentalists as well, though they may reasonably hope to have longer careers. People – Nordica wrote – do not realize 'what it is to come out before the public and in its presence then and there compete for one's position'. Writers and painters work alone and do not as a rule hear comments on their work:

with singers, side by side, there is applause or silence ... The singer is obliged to prove her art on sight ... She receives the verdict of the public in the very moment of production. It is exactly like any other trial of skill, and with the vanquished the situation is a hard one to sustain stoically. Consequently, singers are keenly sensitive to their position.

The hierarchical social structure of eighteenth-century Italy enhanced this competitiveness. Music-making was so organized as to give a few star musicians near-equal footing; but even within this top echelon there must be no confusion about who came ahead of whom. Should the singer of a *seconda parte* (which at that time meant a substantial part, second only to the leading castrato or the prima donna) be allowed an aria with violin obbligato if the *prima parte* had none? Should the leader of the orchestra take his cue for an aria from the chief répétiteur at the harpsichord or from the singer? Such questions of professional etiquette (*convenienze*) were submitted to Padre Martini, the great musicologist, who found ways of dodging them gracefully. To avoid disputes over billing, singers' names were sometimes printed across each other or fanwise, a practice continued here and there into the next century. The dark side of this rivalry was the occasional violent episode, as when the celebrated but notoriously bad-tempered Caffarelli and another castrato beat each other up in church with a double-bass bow and a stick. Most musicians behaved better than that, and we should not take the easy way of dismissing it all as absurd; where rank and precedence were the stuff of society, musicians who fretted about their billing were defending their earning power.

In the nineteenth century there was still a good deal of argument about *convenienze*; as late as the 1880s the carriage that took the singers at the Turin opera to and from rehearsal still had to pick them up and set them down in hierarchical order. The arrival of a full-blown market for musical employment, however, tended to make fees rather than declared status the crucial test; Napoleonic rule blew away some of the more formal distinctions.

In the early eighteenth century nearly all leading musicians, and some humbler ones, had been in the employ of rulers or great nobles. Their employment might be fictitious – some small courts gave out patents as a form of prestige advertising – but it was still thought to confer honour and protection. By about 1750 there were far fewer virtuosos 'belonging' to this or that prince; engagements had so multiplied as to bring about a market, that is, a complex network along which supply of musicians could approximately satisfy the varied array of demands for their services, at many different levels of quality and pay.

The Napoleonic period finished off the old royal patronage of leading musicians; Napoleon himself was the last Italian sovereign to have a Paisiello as his court composer and a leading soprano (the castrato Girolamo Crescentini) as his court singer. Afterwards there were still musicians attached to Italian courts, but the ones that were permanently attached were now exceedingly minor artists; leading musicians might be glad of a nominal court appointment, as Giuseppina Strepponi was of a post at the court of Parma, but it made little or no difference to their busy schedules. Because monarchs and nobles still controlled theatres and orchestras, artists had to use deferential language to them; but that did not prevent them from engaging themselves to the highest bidder. As the father of a prima donna put it in 1823, when she was offered an engagement that supposedly conferred honour but not much money, 'I am concerned with realities, not with chimaeras'. Where a management paid really well, as at Havana, *prima parte* singers could after all bring themselves to take on a *seconda parte*.

Titles now mattered less. Too much importance was attached to them and hence ultimately they were devalued. Rossini at Naples, together with the impresario Domenico Barbaja, was still trying in 1822 to insist that the word *assoluto* or *assoluta* could apply only to one person in each category. This logical argument was soon flouted; every singer or dancer of a part not obviously subordinate was now 'absolute'; what had previously been described as a *seconda donna* become an *altra* ('other') *prima donna*, while a *seconda donna* now had a mere bit part. 'All chiefs and no Indians' meant that cash was the real test – or, as an impresario put it, 'price is the thermometer'.

Working within such a market meant several things: you did your best to keep up your monetary value in comparison with others deemed your equals; you kept watch on those equals for signs that they might be covertly undermining your standing; you relied increasingly on the courts to enforce your contractual rights and, finally, you strove to keep up your bargaining position by showing again and again that your conduct was proper while your negotiating partner's fell sadly short.

Keeping up your monetary value called for the bargaining methods of the bazaar. These differed little whether the parties were modest small-town violinists or internationally known singers. It was generally understood that the potential employer would begin by offering less than he was prepared to pay, the potential employee by demanding more than he or she was willing to settle for; from a leading singer, who might be quoting tens of thousands of francs, this opening demand was referred to as a 'broadside' (*cannonata*). The two sides might or might not then come together in a series of steps.

For the important trade fair season at Senigallia, in 1836, the impresario Alessandro Lanari wished to get a particular cellist; he told his local agent to offer 26 scudi and was prepared to go up to 30. The cellist, however, demanded 50 scudi and eventually came down to 44. The gap was too wide: even in a slack season the cellist was unwilling to spoil his market value. In this he was no different from a leading singer like Carolina Unger, who would not take less than an impresario had paid Giulia Grisi; her 'self-esteem' was involved. Very few artists could exact and then defend a fee that set an Italian record; Bellini achieved this with *La sonnambula* (1831), Verdi with *Macbeth* (1847). Three women superstars – Pasta, Malibran and the then equally admired Giuseppina Ronzi – in the 1830s achieved an Italian record fee of 1,000 francs per performance that was not surpassed until the 1870s. They could all make more money abroad, but within Italy they were keen to make the 1,000-franc standard stick; rather than take less in a relatively small theatre, Ronzi threw in two performances for nothing.

The vast majority, however, still had to establish their market quotation each time through bazaar bargaining. This system ruled the Italian musical world for many yeas, in rather more expeditious form down to the Second World War. Only the coming of a modern industrial economy has superseded it.

Where so many artists were striking bargains at the same time, and everyone's quotation depended on his or her keeping up or bettering a previous standard, it is not surprising that many kept a jealous watch on their competitors. Bellini has become notorious for his deep suspicion of nearly everyone he dealt with in the musical world; he wondered if they were about to do him down, and some have called him paranoid (largely because he confided his innermost thoughts in letters to his intimate friend, who kept and in the end published them). Verdi too was apt to think the worst of his fellows, and to jump down their throats in correspondence, sometimes with reason, sometimes not; but he was either more controlled than Bellini or he kept his stream of consciousness for domestic chats with Giuseppina. He and Donizetti both railed against the 'corrupt' world of opera, but in practice were in no hurry to give it up.

Singers are known for their jealousy of each other. It cannot be denied that there are many examples. Take Lorenza Correa, a strong-minded Spaniard (she needed to be strong-minded, for she was married to the violent-tempered tenor Manuel García). In 1814 she was singing at La Scala alongside the well-known soprano Francesca Festa-Maffei. Correa poured out her grievances to a colleague, switching, in her passion, from Italian to her native Spanish. Festa had tried to prevent her from getting the part of Zerlina in *Don Giovanni* and was much mortified that Correa's performance was now earning more applause than hers as Donna Anna. When a new opera by Mayr went into rehearsal, Mayr visited Festa every day at her own house, but he never visited Correa; he, the librettist, and the impresario had most likely been bribed to saddle her with a second-rate part. When Mayr at length appeared at Correa's lodgings with her aria, she pronounced it a 'real Miserere', refused to sing it, and demanded a new one:

This set everyone by the ears, but they couldn't deny me. In the end the aria was changed, and, thinking to do me down, they've ended by doing themselves down. Festa, who has the best part, has gone right into the s—t, while I've been praised to the skies. The opera was liked hardly at all, but my aria went most spendidly ...

Against such rivalry, it is pleasant to find singers co-operating, for example helping each other over benefit performances (though they also liked to put the fact on record). The young

Giuditta Pasta was befriended by two older prima donnas who might have felt threatened (Violante Camporesi and Giuseppina Grassini); it no doubt helped that Pasta was a lady and a nice woman rather than a Spanish termagant. The more usual situation was well captured by Mercadante, reporting on the successful first night of one of his operas:

The audience happy, the composer happy, the company, the orchestra, the chorus, the supers, the management: good for you, good for me, fine, marvellous, it's all your doing, no, it's mine; petty complaints (muttered), embraces, jealousy among the singers owing to the *weight* of applause, because some got more than others, etc. etc. etc.

In the early eighteenth century an artist like Correa who felt wronged would have tried to enlist a royal or noble protector. Thus, an ageing tenor in the employ of the Duke of Modena, who had had a younger man preferred to him for a season at Reggio, within the duchy, wished the duke's secretary to make it known that 'that is not how a prince's servants are to be treated.' (He still did not get the part.) By the early nineteenth century that kind of patronage was only mildly useful. Musicians liked to deal, for instance, with the nobles and well-off lawyers who owned La Fenice, Venice; it was socially agreeable and could sometimes win them minor favours at the expense of the management. But that was as far as it went. Being someone's mistress – we have seen – never made the career of a leading woman singer although it may have influenced débuts and the casting of minor parts.

Even the deterrent powers of great persons now had about them a strong ritual element. Under the old Italian governments the supervisory body could send musicians to prison for a variety of misdemeanours such as quarrelling backstage, refusing to perform or hissing back at the audience. Even stage-hands went to gaol when the wrong piece of scenery came down in mid-act. But imprisonment on such grounds lasted, as a rule, only a few days or sometimes overnight; its purpose was that those arrested (or their friends on their behalf) should express contrition and show who was boss. Someone who did not play by the rules (or did not know of them) could get away with it. The tenor Luigi Mari, at Modena in 1826, would not sing unless his fee was guaranteed on the government subsidy (because he knew the management was about to fail); he went to gaol, still would not sing and got his guarantee. The English soprano Clara Novello, in the same city (a stronghold of despotism at this time), refused to sing on her rest day. When two dragoons came to arrest her she merely laughed: 'Only fancy them trying to frighten me like that.' She did not go to gaol.

What did govern the day-to-day professional lives of musicians was, increasingly, the law of contract. Musicians' contracts went back to the sixteenth century at least. Admission to sing or play in a royal chapel was governed by a full set of rules, but contracts for the new genre of opera were, to begin with, short and imprecise. This imprecision led to all kinds of problems: for instance, how much should a musician be paid if an engagement was cut short by the ruler's death? Throughout the eighteenth century, contracts became ever more elaborate, as answers to such questions were worked out and matters that had previously been left to custom were incorporated. By 1800, printed contract forms were in common use; they could be used straightforwardly for engaging minor artists, while leading performers struck out some clauses and added others.

Contracts specified what musicians were to perform, between what dates, how frequently, how much they would be paid and at what intervals, and what benefit performances, if any, they would enjoy. Since opera seasons in particular were organized on a tight schedule by impresarios, many of whom had precarious financial resources or none, many things could and did go wrong; the resulting disputes tended more and more to be resolved in the courts.

Despotic though the old Italian states were, they did have civil laws which, on the whole, were allowed to take their course. Before the unification of Italy in 1859–60 the courts themselves can be seen moving gradually away from upholding the general interest as they understood it and towards stricter enforcement of the letter of contracts – in other words, towards a liberal individualist view of law. They could go into musical questions in extraordinary detail, as in a lengthy 1873 judgment, according to which, a management, having engaged the noted Adelaide

Borghi-Mamo as a contralto, had no right to make her sing mezzo-soprano parts, even though they lay within her compass.

For musicians a contract had value not just because it defined their rights but because it could be produced in future negotiations as evidence of their standing in the market. If the musician had consented, for whatever reason, to take less pay or to perform more often than usual, this needed to be disguised: lower pay was termed a 'present' rather than a 'fee'; a leading singer like Erminia Frezzolini was prepared to give extra performances, but only 'on her honour'; there must be no mention of them in her contract.

A final rule of survival in the musical bazaar was that when negotiating you must play up both your merits and your grievances so as to put the other party at a disadvantage. Donizetti's letter to Lanari, already quoted, is an example:

You speak to me of *friendship*, of *esteem* etc. – what are you on about? If you have shown me friendship, I have shown it you; if you esteem me, I esteem you, but what you have never yet given me, and I have given you, is proof of disinterestedness.

Donizetti went on to detail his 'proof': he had been willing to compose *Parisina* in a rush even though the delay over the libretto had entitled him to break the contract and still get paid; he had agreed, as 'an honourable, disinterested friend who esteems you', to take deferred payment; he had rehearsed the opera and even corrected the proofs of the libretto. He then summoned Lanari for the last time to tell him whether he wanted him for the carnival season of 1834, and if not to pay compensation. 'The courts do not frighten me, and I shall always be in any case, Your

GAETANO DONIZETTI'.

To an English-speaking reader this letter may sound more boastful than it really is. Many Italians, to this day, are prepared to blow their own trumpet without feeling the need to mask it by indirection or self-deprecatory humour. Donizetti was really just using the jargon of his trade. 'Friendship' and 'esteem' denoted business relationships, not personal feelings; we can find musicians describing as a 'friend' a person they had yet to meet. It meant someone who did what you asked. Failure to do so showed a lack of friendship, to be countered by a list of the 'sacrifices' you had made, and an explicit request for those 'sacrifices' to be matched by the other party. The recriminatory, tit-for-tat burden of much early nineteenth-century musical correspondence was highly conventional – a sign of general strain rather than of private ill-feeling, although there may, at times, have been ill-feeling as well.

The strain told on individuals. Verdi repeatedly complained of his 'years in the galleys' before *Rigoletto*, *Il trovatore* and *La traviata* brought him unparalleled success and allowed him to work at greater leisure. Yet his rate of composition – two operas a year – was well below Donizetti's or Pacini's. It was still more than he could cope with healthily; his acute stomach pains were probably psychosomatic.

Singers now and then talked of retiring early, and some meant it – women perhaps more often than men. This was still a time when the manager of the King's Theatre in the Haymarket assumed that 'the only object which can induce a woman of character and education to come on the stage' (he was thinking of Violante Camporesi) was 'the hope of emolument'. Camporesi, at the age of 34, thought of getting out, though she was still singing – and talking of retiring – eight years later. Giuditta Pasta at 29 thought of retiring in three years' time – she was making a lot of money in London and Paris, and she liked the idea of going straight from singing the parts of tragic queens to being a 'country girl' at the villa she had just bought on Lake Como. If she went on longer, it was probably (in her unfortunate late comebacks certainly) because her investments had gone wrong.

Other women singers escaped by way of marriage into the nobility. In Italy this had been frowned upon or even prohibited before the late eighteenth century, but the new (relative) respectability, together with a star singer's earning power, opened doors. Ester Mombelli, Adelaide Tosi, Marietta Gazzaniga, Marietta Alboni, the German Henriette Sontag and the Englishwoman Clara Novello all married Italian nobles, though some had to go back to work when political or financial troubles blew up. There were to be many more such marriages.

The average small-part singer or locally based instrumentalist had no such escape route. How most of them ended their careers we do not know; clearly, many fell into poverty.

Those good enough or lucky enough to be on an official musical establishment might, as we have seen, go on drawing half pay when they were no longer able to perform; this was the system in a number of north Italian municipal orchestras. The Naples royal establishments had an official pension scheme, but it was actuarially primitive and, like the Naples government in general, often paid late, sometimes years late; in the 1830s and 1840s newly retired musicians had to wait for a vacancy, that is, for existing pensioners to die off.

Musicians in Naples could also belong to a religious confraternity that acted as a mutual benefit society providing medical treatment, funeral expenses and masses for the deceased member's soul. This body, which went back at least as far as 1649 and was still in being in 1878, was one of a number of such societies up and down the peninsula. It admitted men only, most of them ordinary, locally based musicians; from 1826 there were limited facilities for members' women relatives. The society had tried, in the 1790s, to set itself up as a guild working a closed shop, without apparent success. At various times it declared its intention of providing members with some kind of pension if financial resources allowed, but there is no sign that much came of this plan. There were also, no doubt, musicians in the lower reaches of the Naples musical world who could not afford its subscription. At this level, a superannuated musician readily turned into a beggar.

PART TWO

6 Revolution and Unity

Verdi was the representative Italian musician of the nineteenth century – in some ways; in others he was unique. His experience of the great political crisis which Italy lived through at mid-century shows him evolving just as numbers of other liberal-minded Italians evolved.

In the early 1840s, as we have seen, Verdi's work spoke for a strong sense of collective identity and aspiration, and an equally strong need to discharge a pent-up heroic energy. It did not, however, draw or even hint at any specific political conclusion. At this stage Verdi may be called a nationalist in the general sense that he looked to the Italian people to assert their identity and redeem themselves from political oppression; but we should beware of reading back into his early outlook (or into that of many other Italians) a strong desire for the establishment of a unitary Italian state. Once that state had come into being, in ways that the young Verdi might not have approved, nearly everyone became persuaded that they had always longed for it.

It is unclear how far Verdi shared in the political ferment that overtook Italy from 1846. What we do know is that when revolution broke out in 1848 all over Italy (and over much of Europe) he wrote of his joy and relief at seeing the country freed from oppressive rule: 'Honour to all Italy, which at this moment is really great! Be assured, her hour of liberation has come. It is the people who demand it, and there is no absolute power that can resist the will of the people.'

Verdi himself, however, spent much of 1848 in Paris, where he had business interests. When he did go to Italy, it was again on business, to buy an estate near the modest home where he had grown up. Nonetheless, he met Mazzini, the apostle of liberation through the collective self-sacrificing action of the people, and was clearly influenced by him for a time; he became persuaded that Italy was about to become a free, united republic; at Mazzini's request he wrote a national anthem. A little later, he composed a patriotic opera, *La battaglia di Legnano*, for performance in the 1849 Roman republic presided over by Mazzini and defended by Garibaldi. By the time it was performed, Milan had already fallen to a revived Austrian army, and Verdi agreed, as a temporary measure, to let *La battaglia* be performed there and elsewhere with an altered, non-Italian subject and title: an understandable step for him and his Milan-based publisher to take, but hardly the gesture of a do-or-die nationalist.

At the next main crisis of Italian independence, in 1859–60, Verdi was again captivated, this time by Cavour, the statesman whose aim had been not Mazzinian revolution in universal republican brotherhood but the modernization and prudent aggrandisement of the Piedmontese monarchy. Cavour's brand of moderate liberalism seems to have remained Verdi's ideal for the rest of his life. It meant moving towards enlightenment, efficiency, freedom from clerical interference and a government representative of the educated and propertied classes, rather than popular democracy, and certainly nothing like redistribution or collective control of wealth.

The world of Italian art–music had been closely bound up with the old ruling élites of the various states. For most musicians, this was a matter of economic necessity rather than of ideology. Verdi claimed not to understand politics; he may not have given it sustained attention, but he certainly understood it better than many of his colleagues. The majority were perhaps closer in their behaviour to the Tuscan Teodulo Mabellini. This respectable composer and teacher wrote a cantata in 1847 to celebrate the grand-duke's assent to the formation of a civic guard – a middle-class volunteer force, and a clear prelude to the granting of a constitution; in 1849 he wrote another cantata to mark the grand-duke's return on the back of the Austrian army. Mabellini was nothing so dramatic as a turncoat – only a musician getting on with the job.

Verdi's own shifts of mood and allegiance, from an early belief in an austere ideal of liberty patterned after the ancient Roman republic, to temporary fervour for spontaneous national liberation on the Mazzinian model, to settled adherence to moderate liberalism and parliamentary government under the Piedmontese crown, matched those of a good many thinking Italians. They raise the question: how far was the musical world as a whole identified with the new élite of united liberal Italy as it emerged from the wars of independence?

That élite was, for many years, hemmed in between two numerically stronger forces. On the one hand were, at all times, the poverty-stricken peasant masses and the Roman Catholic church which the course of the *risorgimento* had alienated; on the other hand there stood, to begin with, an artisan class which, in parts of Italy, had strong Mazzinian and democratic leanings, later flanked by an emergent industrial working class with militant trade unions and socialist or anarcho-syndicalist organizations. The rule of the liberal élite between 1860 and 1922 has drawn strong criticism from some recent English-speaking commentators; David Pryce-Jones has described Italy in this period as 'rotten from top to bottom', a remarkable statement to have come, in 1989, from a noted historian and biographer. In Italy too, though as a rule in more measured terms, the old liberal élite has come in for obloquy. What were and are the reasons for disappointment?

Late Victorian Britain could draw on a long tradition of support for Italian liberty and independence. Poets from Byron to Swinburne hymned it, statesmen like Lord John Russell and Gladstone forwarded it. Britain as the heartland of liberalism could show unreserved support for a 'people rightly struggling to be free', an attitude found not only among the educated but in the London working and lower middle classes too, an estimated three-quarters of a million of whom turned out to welcome Garibaldi in 1864. Behind this lay not only the radicals' hatred of tyranny and clericalism but a vicarious pleasure in revolutionary violence that could not be resorted to at home; there was a brisk trade in handkerchiefs said to have been steeped in blood from Garibaldi's wounds. For the British élite, however, Italy represented much more; it was still the home of the classical antiquity on which they had been brought up and an acquaintance with its modern language and literature, art and music, was a fit attainment for an educated person. Disraeli and Gladstone both read Dante in the original, though Gladstone went further and read new Italian works of philosophy, for instance, as they came out.

There was some carry-over after unification, as the myth became established of an independence movement or *risorgimento* in which Cavour, Mazzini and Garibaldi had somehow co-operated to bring about an Italy united under the Piedmontese monarchy, even though the three had, at most times, been fiercely at odds with one another over both ends and means. The young historian G. M. Trevelyan paced over the sites of Garibaldi's skirmishes and marches, and brought out, shortly before the First World War, a popular trilogy. In the same generation and in much the same spirit, the Oxford under-graduate Clement Attlee studied Italian and thus became almost certainly the last British Prime Minister in history to be acquainted with the language.

The new Italy could now be visited by train much more easily than in the past; tunnels were made through the Alps, with much loss of workmen's lives; under Mont Cenis in 1876 and under the St Gotthard in 1884. But to the thoughtful visitor it seemed, in many ways, a comedown from the legendary days of the struggle for independence. If that struggle had not been turned into a myth – perhaps unavoidable in a doubtfully cohesive new country, brought into being by a determined minority – the actual Italy might not have seemed so disappointing. The sense of falling short of a glorious ideal comes through strongly in the peroration to Bolton King's *History of Italian Unity* (1899), a book by a Birmingham liberal radical that was widely influential.

United Italy, he acknowledged, had done away with police spies, ecclesiastical tyranny and official obscurantism. Average

2. The apotheosis of the nineteenth-century Italian opera house: the Teatro Colón, Buenos Aires (1908), built and originally managed by Italians

3. An all-Italian popular opera house overseas: the Teatro Marconi, Buenos Aires (1903; originally the Doria; destroyed *c.* 1960). The sign at the extreme right is that of the Gran Café Paganini

1. (*Previous page*): The tarantella. A somewhat idealized nineteenth-century lithograph, Museo di S. Martino, Naples

4. Giuditta Pasta as Anna Bolena in Donizetti's opera, 1830,
by Brulon

5a & b. Arnaldo Tedeschi in costume as Manrico in a
children's opera company, *c.* 1904 (he did not sing the
complete opera but appeared between the acts of comic
operas to sing 'Di quella pira')

6. A product of local patriotism: a postcard showing the two leading tenors born in Montagnana, near Padua (Aureliano Pertile, left, as Nero in Boito's opera, Giovanni Martinelli, right, as Eléazar in Halévy's *La Juive*)

7. A setting for a romantic ballet: *Ettore Fieramosca*, Teatro San Carlo, 1837

8. (*Left*): A tambourine seller, Naples,
Museo di S. Martino

9. (*Above*): A bagpipe player: sketch by
Servitelli, Museo di S. Martino, Naples

10. (*Right*): Another bagpipe player, by
De Vito, Museo di S. Martino, Naples

11. Unknown singer in a Scottish part, *c.* 1830

12. The popular comic singer, Nicola Maldacea: postcard put out by the
Naples publisher, Bideri

13. Street musicians in Venice noisily seeing in the new year

16. The band of the Società Lago di Como, an Italian mutual aid society in Buenos Aires, *c.* 1898

17. The (virtually all-Italian) municipal band of Buenos Aires, *c.* 1930

14. (*Opposite top*): Setting by Antonio Niccolini for the final scene of Rossini's *Semiramide*, Teatro San Carlo, Naples, 1823: Museo di S. Martino, Naples

15. (*Opposite bottom*): A masked ball at the Teatro San Carlo, Naples

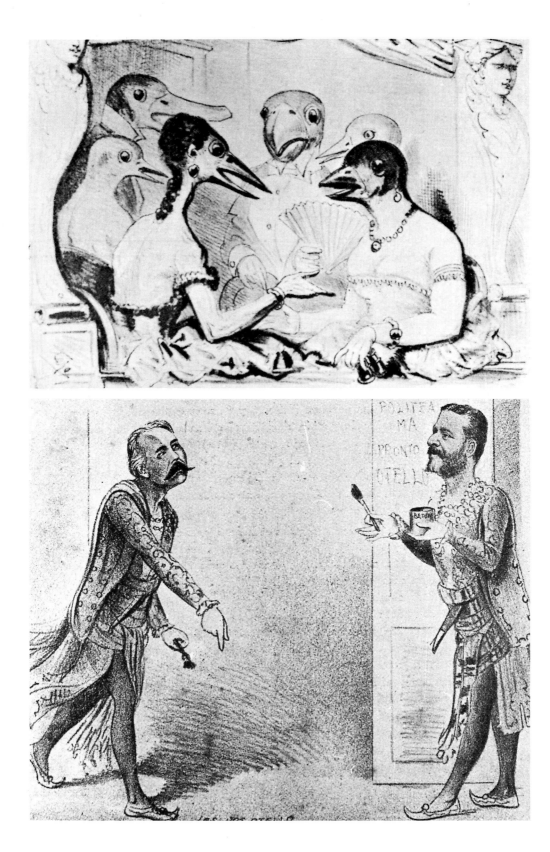

18. (*Opposite top*): A cartoon satirizing the noisy habits of Italian opera-goers, from the Turin journal *Pasquino*, 1876 (no. 2), reproduced in G. Depanis, *I concerti popolari ed il Teatro Regio di Torino* (Turin, 1914-15), I, facing p. 100. The caption (not reproduced here), after giving a number of bird noises, comments 'And this is how you are supposed to hear opera in the land that gave it birth!'

19. (*Opposite bottom*): The Italian impresarios Angelo Ferrari and Cesare Ciacchi. Both put on *Otello* in Buenos Aires in 1888, within a year of the Milan first performance; Ferrari had the rights, but in the absence of effective Argentine copyright Ciacchi got in first (contemporary cartoon)

20. (*Above*): Nineteenth-century presses used by the music publisher Ricordi

21. Title page of an oratorio by the priest-composer Lorenzo Perosi

22. An office at the music publishing home of Ricordi

23. (*Following page*): Early nineteenth-century carnival in Rome

life expectancy had risen; railways had been built; industry had grown remarkably; savings banks and mutual aid societies had grown likewise; Italians were aware of being members of a great state and of counting for something in the world. On the other hand, Italy was burdened with 'her grinding poverty, the unreality of her political life, the spiritual vulture that gnaws at her vitals'. (We will consider later what that vulture might have been.) She lacked 'religion . . . the puritanism of her great Ricasoli [an upright aristocratic leader of the *risorgimento*] . . . the constraining sense of duty that Mazzini preached'. She ought to care more for freedom and for the deprived. She needed 'to keep clear of the temptations of a great power, to renounce charlatanry and adventure and militarism, to forswear showy ambitions that only drain her strength.'

Much of what King described had come to everyone's notice in the late 1880s and 1890s. Industrial growth in particular was very recent – still largely confined to the north-west, but striking. His strictures on militarism and on overseas adventures, and his hints at repression at home, were aimed at Francesco Crispi's and later governments which had engaged in all those things, latterly with disastrous results – a stunning defeat at the hands of Abyssinia, and the shooting down of demonstrators in Milan by the army.

Almost immediately after the publication of King's book, Italy turned a corner and entered a turbulent period of growth, moving towards universal manhood suffrage (attained in 1913) and the beginnings of modern social legislation under the liberal governments of Giovanni Giolitti. Some have drawn a rough comparison with the British Liberal governments of 1906–14 dominated by Asquith and Lloyd George, but King, in the 1924 edition of his book, took the opposite line (as many of his radical persuasion have) and denounced Giolitti's 'feeble and corrupt system, masquerading as parliamentary government'.

What followed next, after the profound shock of the First World War, was the 20-year experience of Fascism, and the question has ever since had to be asked: did Fascism represent a sharp break in the history of modern Italy (a thesis put forward by the historian and philosopher Benedetto Croce) or did it, on the contrary, follow on from the political and social workings, the habits of mind and the structural deficiencies of liberal Italy (a view worked out by the early Communist thinker Antonio Gramsci, and carried forward from different premises by the modern historian Denis Mack Smith among others)?

The question cannot be pursued here. Its roots, and those of liberal Italy itself, lay in the 1848–9 revolutions. The initial success of the revolutions marked a high point of idealism among those who took part; their failure compelled many to think out afresh their view of the world.

Revolutionaries in 1848 were still a minority, though there were genuine popular risings, for instance in Milan and Venice. The ideals which different groups pursued varied widely and were often at odds with one another. Some wanted a united Italian republic, some (as in Venice) the return of local independence, some a federal Italy preserving the autonomy of the existing states; all these might harbour deep suspicions of the only native Italian dynasty with a regular armed force, that of Piedmont, which espoused the independence movement as a means of extending its territories. There were further divisions between moderate aristocratic and bourgeois groups on the one hand and democratic groups based on artisans and some intellectuals on the other.

The upshot was disaster as the Austrian armies rallied, defeated the Piedmontese, and restored the old sovereigns. Constitutions reluctantly granted were hastily withdrawn – everywhere except Piedmont. Governments which had always been despotic now had more serious grounds than ever for fearing subversion; in opera, censorship became a real nuisance.

Yet the revolutions had shaken the old order irretrievably. States shown to be utterly dependent on foreign powers, Austria and France (which had themselves undergone upheaval in 1848), no longer drew the intimate loyalties of most educated people. The old local élites could no longer be sure of their own place or satisfy others' expectations. The nation state, with industry and education as its base, seemed the right way for a people to organize its collective life; even in Naples and Sicily, where people going north had often been said to be 'going to Italy', an

Italian destiny now seemed, to many of the educated, both inevitable and right.

At the same time, the defeat of so many illusions suggested the need for a more realistic outlook. Armed might and shrewd diplomacy, not spontaneous revolution, would bring about a better order. 'Blood and iron' was how Bismarck put it in Germany. In Italy it meant a less dramatic reliance on Piedmontese forces and on playing off Italy's stronger neighbours against each other. More widely, the rise of apparently objective scientific disciplines, and in particular the doctrine of evolution through the survival of the fittest, seemed to show that individuals and nations could thrive only through toughness and through reliance on hard facts. As the great Lord Salisbury, the late Victorian Prime Minister, once put it, 'I want the dynamics, not the ethics of the question'. Lord Salisbury reconciled this with his profound Christian faith by stressing the pessimistic side of Christianity; so fallen was human nature that in this world one could fight fire only with fire. Among the élite of liberal Italy, few of whom were active Christians (because the church was still hostile to the new nation, root and branch), some found it easier still to adopt an ethic of cleverness and power.

However, it was not easy to display power in a militarily weak country which twice (in 1859 and 1866) had to acquire vital territories by being handed them on a plate by France and Prussia, and later (1870) acquired Rome when those same powers were busy fighting each other. The last third of the century saw the rise of great modern cities – Milan, Turin, Genoa and Rome – with railways, trams, modern shops and offices, and apartment blocks on the model of boulevard Paris; but it was difficult to believe in the modernity and cohesion of the nation as a whole, when for the first ten years a virtual peasant war against the new state raged in parts of the south, and when, later still, the poverty and squalor of Naples were shown up in the 1884 and 1910–11 cholera epidemics.

One reaction was to condemn the narrow élites that had run the old states, and even the not much wider ones that had brought the new Italy into being and had run it in its formative years. Already, almost from unification, precepts of economic liberalism had come in and dictated savings in government expenditure on what appeared to be luxuries. From 1876 a more middle-class, somewhat more democratically inclined grouping was dominant in politics, and from 1882 rather more people, though still a small minority, had the vote. All this, as we shall see, was quite enough to precipitate a crisis in the financing of music.

Another way of coping with the inadequacy of the new Italy was to proclaim the unexampled superiority of the Italian people: their civilization, their art, their innate qualities of energy, daring and imagination. The poet Giosuè Carducci, in many ways still a traditional *risorgimento* figure, in a celebrated ode, rediscovered among the clear Apennine springs the pagan joys of antiquity, which, in his view, centuries of Catholicism had overlaid. The next great poet, Gabriele d'Annunzio, himself very much in the pagan joys line, urged, in powerful lyrics, the cult of energy, sensation and sensuality, both upon individuals and upon the nation; he reinvented a poetic language based, in part, on medievalisms and, like other aesthetes of the period, revelled in images of blood and death. Both poets in their different ways showed contempt for the pettiness of the new bourgeois society around them.

That society read them both avidly and was profoundly influenced by D'Annunzio in particular. (He and his school may have been the 'spiritual vulture' Bolton King saw gnawing at Italy's vitals.) There had long been a national culture of the upper classes, but with the widening of the middle class – still largely made up of professionals, officials and white-collar workers, rather than of industrial managers – the national culture spread to far more people. There were now newspapers and journals with respectable circulations (though there was not, and never yet has been, a popular mass-circulation daily press on the London or Paris model). Far more novels were published and read than in the first half of the century. Yet, although the national culture was wider than in the past, it was also much less influential abroad (opera excepted), and much more receptive to foreign influences: French naturalism and aestheticism, German Hegelianism, eventually Marxism, all swept in and found many disciples. Bourgeois taste now counted, but bourgeois taste was at once uncertain and often overblown.

This still shows in the public monuments of the period. Foreign visitors often imagine Milan central station and the Victor Emmanuel monument in Rome to be examples of Fascist architecture; both were, in fact, designed before the First World War. They represent, on the grossest scale, the 'Umbertino' style, roughly coinciding with the reign of King Umberto I (1878–1900). It is still found in many buildings and in extravagant statuary unmatched elsewhere in Europe, some grandiloquent, some with sado-masochistic overtones (involving voluptuous women and animals, or animals fighting each other). The squares of Turin, and the Montagnola park at Bologna, provide striking examples.

Music, one might think, would be immune from all this rhetoric, for the usual reason that music is imprecise and ambiguous in conveying ideas or even feelings. But, in its own way, music followed the general trend.

Musicians could bang the nationalist drum in praise of the supposed Italian qualities of Italian music. In the early nineteenth century the almost automatic charge of 'German pedantry' levelled at composers who tried something new by way of orchestration spoke not for nationalism, but for the old-fashioned belief in the centrality of all the Italian arts. Rossini heeded the criticism, on the whole, not just to be popular but because the self-confidence of Italian musicians and audiences was such as to make an Italianate musical language still the most viable, with minor innovations here and there to bring piquancy and interest. By the 1860s this self-confidence was ebbing fast, and the temptation to mount a nationalistic counter-offensive was growing.

The most notorious sign of waning self-confidence is Arrigo Boito's poem of 1863, in which he called upon a musician and fellow-member of the 'scapigliato' ('dishevelled') movement to restore the altar of Italian art, 'now befouled like the walls of a brothel' – an expression which deeply wounded Verdi, the leading Italian musician. The 'dishevelled ones' were followers of French Romanticism, especially of Victor Hugo, with an added taste of their own for the sinister and the grotesque; they were themselves a token of the new Italian openness to foreign influences.

In the 1860s and 1870s the chief musical influence was French – first Meyerbeer, then Gounod and later Massenet. A little later, especially after the first Italian performance of *Lohengrin* (Bologna, 1871), the great topic of dispute was 'Wagnerism', often used as an umbrella term to cover all departures from the accustomed formal structures of music. Wagner's own works, the popular *Lohengrin* apart, took longer to arrive. *Tristan und Isolde*, the fount of modern music, waited until 1888 for its first Italian performance (again at Bologna), and Wagner did not become a staple until near the turn of the century.

These influences were, on the one hand, accepted – as those of Mozart and Beethoven had not been in the early years of the century, unless by small minorities. Meyerbeer's music was upheld by the young critic Abramo Basevi (who went on to write a pioneer study of Verdi) as 'the living expression of new needs'; his Paris grand operas were performed, sometimes at considerable expense, and were regarded as special occasions – *Le Prophète*, for instance, was given at Venice, with an extra subsidy, in honour of an all-Italian scientific congress. Massenet's early grand operas (*Le Roi de Lahore* and *Hérodiade*) and his later sentimental operas (*Manon* and *Werther*) were influential, the former in encouraging a cult of the exotic, the latter through their combination of elegance, lyrical feeling and cleverly tinted orchestration. In the end, Wagner carried nearly all before him, at least among the intellectuals, though there was some resistance. At Naples in the 1890s – intellectually a much more important city than its wretched economic and social condition might suggest – a well-informed and progressive-minded little group of critics, headed by Michele Uda, instilled into their readers a high regard not only for Wagner but for Ibsen too.

On the other hand, the influential critic Francesco D'Arcais repeatedly bemoaned what he saw as the de-Italianizing of Italian music. In an obituary of Ponchielli (a composer he did not think very highly of) he complained, in 1886, that eclecticism and especially Germanism – the example of Wagner in particular – were all that young composers wanted to pursue. Verdi, he wrote, was admired but little followed; the essence of Italian music, which he still understood to be melodic invention, was being lost. On the international artistic exchange 'Italy gives little and takes much'. She had gained politically, attaining the dignity of nationhood, and was moving towards prosperity, but 'in the arts and letters, on the other hand, she has become more than ever a servant and slave of other peoples'.

Verdi, in theory, shared this view. He said again and again that German symphonic music was fine for non-Italians, but Italian composers should stick to the traditional virtues of Italian music and not go haring after 'scientific' novelties. His famous saying 'let's go back to the old – it will be a step forward' seems to have meant that young musicians should study a select list of Italian composers from Palestrina on.

What such studies would do for Italian music was not quite clear. Verdi himself was the least traditionalist of composers. He remained highly innovative, moving forward from work to work through a career of half a century. But it was understandably annoying to him that every advance, individual though it remained, should have been greeted with cries of 'Wagnerism'. Verdi sat through the Bologna *Lohengrin* of 1871, scribbling on the libretto 'swan ugly' (not the first or the last time that such a sentiment could have been noted down) as well as several remarks to the effect that the work was too long-winded. The long Wagnerian span was indeed at the opposite extreme from Verdi's ideal of extreme concision. Yet Verdi picked up a great deal, not only from Wagner but from French composers, by way not of imitation but of absorption of harmonic procedures or instrumental colour, which he then totally recreated as part of a new Verdian language. In spite of all this, Verdi remained in his pronouncements on music a grumpy old nationalist.

The challenge of early Italian music was to be taken up in earnest only in the nineteenth century, by the composers of the so-called generation of 1880 (Malipiero, Pizzetti and Casella) who were under the potent influence of D'Annunzio and his slogan 'back to Monteverdi'. This meant rather more than 'back to Palestrina' ever had; it meant, in the first place, a return to the setting of a poetic text unencumbered with heavy orchestration or with most of the paraphernalia of Italian opera as it had developed in the nineteenth century. In the event it also meant the arrival of a permanent avant-garde, unable ever to touch a wide audience. In this, the 'generation of 1880' merely signalled the Italian version of a profound change that overtook all the arts about this time throughout Europe and America.

At about the turn of the nineteenth and twentieth centuries this change was no more than potential. Musicians could still have it both ways, though at considerable hidden cost to themselves.

On the one hand they could denounce the foreign domination of Italian musical life, which was supposedly adulterating Italian music and preventing young Italian composers from being heard. The target was to begin with French music, as when the tenor Roberto Stagno (in a private letter of 1889) criticized the publisher Edoardo Sonzogno as 'that millionaire autocrat ... sold out to the foreigner' for having successfully pushed works by Lalo, Thomas and Massenet on the Italian market. Later, after Wagner had dominated the repertoire at La Scala for over a decade, the first performance there of Richard Strauss's *Der Rosenkavalier* (1911) was greeted with a shower of protest leaflets from the upper gallery.

On the other hand Italian musicians could still revel in all manner of exotic novelties imported from abroad, mainly from France. The career of Pietro Mascagni is a case in point.

The instantaneous success of *Cavalleria rusticana* at the very start of the 1890s made him the leader of the 'young school' that came to vivid notice in that decade (its other leading members were Giordano, Cilea and Leoncavallo; Puccini was erroneously lumped in with them at the time and for a good while after).

At the time of *Cavalleria* Mascagni had not had time to become self-conscious; the work has often been called crude in its harmonic procedures, yet its spontaneous poster-like lyricism, rooted in popular song and popular opera, carries all before it. Then Mascagni woke up famous; he took to culture and refinement. In *L'amico Fritz* (1891) his dallying with a French taste for charm and local colour brought off one or two pretty moments, but (as Shaw wrote) 'the rest is more artificial [than *Cavalleria*] without being in any way better, except that the orchestra is more knowingly handled'. By the time of *Iris* (1898), Mascagni was taking on simultaneously the French naturalists' taste for sleaze and the French sentimentalists' taste for the Orient (the Japanese heroine is abducted into a brothel and commits suicide in a sewer) while the 'knowingness' of his orchestration was veering towards the overblown and his lyrical melodic gift was losing focus. His remaining work was a string of ambitious operas for some of which a case is now and then mounted in Italy; none, however, has made its way elsewhere. Mascagni thought of himself at one time as a socialist, then as a suitable collaborator of D'Annunzio, in the end as a fascist; though talented and in some ways a generous personality, he remained an egocentric muddler out of his depth.

Mascagni's fate seems the outcome not just of personal failings but of the contradictions within Italian culture in his formative years. How his near contemporary Puccini managed to make something lasting out of those contradictions will be dealt with in a later chapter. What now impresses is how singular Puccini was in his day – a time when lack of a clear Italian identity made for stridency and confusion.

7 A Musical Nation?

Was united Italy still *the* musical nation? Was it indeed a musical nation?

Most people in the last third of the nineteenth century had no doubt of the answer, so far as they bothered to think about it. Modern Italy might no longer be supreme in painting and sculpture: that much had sunk in, though the accumulated capital of the Italian fine arts was so vast, and tourists were so eager to take it in, that it cast a halo over the country's relatively modest nineteenth-century achievement. But in music? Was not Italian opera dominant in all civilized countries? At Covent Garden as late as 1888 even so quintessentially Germanic a work as *Die Meistersinger* was performed in Italian as a matter of course; for was not Italian the natural, the unavoidable language of opera? So firmly rooted was this cliché that outside Italy, to this day, the cartoonist's shorthand for an Italian is an enthusiast with a black moustache, ready at any moment to burst into an aria; waiters in the more dubious Italian restaurants trade on it by indulging in familiar backslapping, interspersed with snatches of song, which they would never risk in Italy itself.

A thoughtful minority of Italians, however, could not rest content with things as they were in the newly united kingdom. Many of their worries were summed up in 1877 by Michele Ruta, a cultivated Neapolitan musician who taught in the city's music school (*Conservatorio*) and ultimately became its head. In a critical essay on the condition of music in Italy, he drew up a sort of decalogue of all that was wrong.

The contrast he drew was with other countries, Germany in particular. There were in Italy no schools of choral singing, or at least the schools that did exist were very poorly organized and supported. Popular music – he had Neapolitan song in mind – was corrupting taste and morals. Itinerant musicians had become a plague, through the obscenity of their songs in particular. Concerts were little encouraged and ill attended. Sheet music was expensive, and for Italian classical music you had to go to German publishers. Sacred music had fallen very low; with women still not allowed to take part, it now lacked high voices, and the Italian school of organ music had perished. Chamber music was lovingly cultivated by some, but too much operatic influence got into it. In the making of musical instruments Italians could no longer compete with foreigners. Teaching methods were now drawn from France and Germany. In opera, too much was taken from the 'immoral' side of French *opéra-comique*, and the vogue for French operas themselves was spoiling young Italian composers' chances. It was all, he wrote, a melancholy contrast with what the musicologist Charles Burney had heard during his celebrated Italian journey in 1770. Besides this list of national failings, Ruta had a series of complaints about the Naples music school, which could be summed up as a lack both of collective spirit in ensemble music and of a broadening humane education.

Ruta's critique mirrored the attitudes of many educated Italians. Like him, they felt ashamed of the old Italy, surviving as it did within the new; it struck them as backward and vulgar. The backwardness showed in the country's reluctance to take up nineteenth-century ideals such as collective self-improvement through popular education; the vulgarity, in its uncivilized habits. The Naples Conservatorio itself, according to Ruta, suffered from a lack of 'moral education' and 'hygienic principles'. He may have had in mind incidents such as a complaint lodged in 1863 by the cleaners at the Teatro San Carlo: during the dress rehearsal of an opera, they alleged, the pupils, together with their supervisor, had urinated in the stalls and the corridors and, when remonstrated with, had given a 'brusque reply'. Ruta now proposed that all the pupils should learn choral singing, and he wished besides to see 'orpheonic societies and temperance choirs' founded among the population at large; the outcome he dreamt of was thousands of voices singing religious or patriotic songs. Within the music school there should be careful training in chamber and orchestral music and a well-developed general education along literary and scientific lines.

Ruta's inspiration is not hard to find. He had absorbed the ideals of Berlioz and many others for whom massed choirs embodied the spirit of progressive humanity. He had adopted the priorities of the German symphonic school, according to which serious orchestral or choral music was the worthiest carrier of public themes, and austere chamber music of private ones. In accordance with the usual nationalist paradox, he had made these foreign ideals his own, while complaining that Italy was too much under foreign influence. In this he was not alone among Italian musicians. But in Naples, the embodiment of the largely unreconstructed old Italy, he had an uphill task. He seems to have made little lasting impression on the Conservatorio. In 1913, a government commissioner reported that the pupils still had to practise in groups amid general cacophony; there had, in other words, been no change since Burney's day (though at the Parma Conservatorio when the young Arturo Toscanini attended it in the early 1880s each boarder had a practice room to himself). The latrines were still dreadful; the building (a delightful rococo ex-convent) was in danger of falling down and had to be shored up, and whether pupils paid fees was decided by 'patriarchal' methods rather than according to the regulations.

Naples, as usual, was an extreme case. In its anarchic vitality it had managed to stave off the coming of nineteenth-century progressive measures, even though it had seen one of the first attempts to put them in place.

Early in the century, the Napoleonic governments of Italy had decided to reform musical education along the lines already adopted in revolutionary France. The most sustained efforts were made in Milan, Bologna and Naples, and it was these that shaped the development of musical education in united Italy –

though we should bear in mind that a great deal of musical training still went on in private, within the family or with individual teachers.

The basic problem, as seen by the new governments of Napoleonic Italy, was that the dissolution of many monastic orders and the break-up of royal or ducal chapels had played havoc with the training of musicians; it had also left many teachers unemployed. The thing to do was to create, in Italy, state teaching institutions like the Paris Conservatoire, itself founded as recently as 1795. A specifically Italian concern was that the new bodies should train, first, singers to sing in the chorus at the opera and secondly, wind players for military or municipal bands.

The chorus in opera had been growing in importance since about 1770, yet – save in one or two places such as Bergamo and Trieste – chorus singers were musically illiterate. Already in 1769 French influence in the person of Du Tillot, the reforming chief minister of the Duke of Parma, had set up a free chorus school; it took pupils of both sexes (a startling innovation in Italy) who would be obliged to sing in the Parma opera house. Du Tillot was an operatic as well as a political reformer, and tried to introduce into Italy the works of Rameau, which called for far more choral singing than Italian audiences were used to. The school was abolished in 1792 on financial grounds, but the need was still felt.

Bands were the craze of the revolutionary and Napoleonic era; they went on tootling and blaring throughout the nineteenth century. In Venice, where Austrian military bands played in St Mark's Square from 1814 to 1866 (with a break during the 1848–9 revolution), the first aim of the state music school, when it was at length set up in 1876, was to train bandsmen for municipal concerts.

For these reasons, state music schools were set up from 1804–8 at Bologna, Naples and Milan; though variously described as *liceo*, *collegio* and *conservatorio*, they all, in the end, came to be known as conservatories, as did other schools founded at Parma (1820), Turin (1827), Venice (various attempts from 1811, culminating in 1876) and elsewhere. For convenience sake we will call them that and ignore the legal and administrative steps by which they changed their status.

They were far from being wholly new institutions. Continuity was such that at Bologna the 89-year-old Lorenzo Gibelli, who had trained several generations of singers, took up in the new school where he had left off, declaring that he felt no need to let someone else take over. There and elsewhere many of the teachers were connected with the local opera house or the philharmonic association or (occasionally still) the church; and the old system of pupil teachers was still in use for many years, at Naples until 1914. But there were significant new features.

Milan, as usual the most advanced, admitted girls from the start – to the singing class only; they were shortly allowed into the piano class as well, but neither here nor in other nineteenth-century institutions could they study other instruments, except for the harp and, very occasionally near the end of the century, the violin and 'cello. Milan, alone of the early nineteenth-century music schools, was to turn out well-known prima donnas such as Giuseppina Strepponi (Verdi's future wife) and the Brambilla sisters. Bologna compromised – girls could have individual lessons at home but must take part in collective rehearsals; Naples, with its Spanish background, got round to admitting them only in 1817 and then only as external students; while a music school at Reggio Calabria, on the very toe of the Italian boot, facing Sicily, in 1832 still did not admit them at all. Even in Milan, care was taken to see that girls and boys attended separate classes; in Turin the classes were held many hours apart, so that boys and girls should not meet even in the corridors. Girls were altogether a problem. At the Venice conservatory in 1883, which hoped to perform a psalm by Marcello in the presence of the visiting Wagner and Liszt, the girls' voices raised 'the usual difficulty'; they were evidently weak, but the only likely source of reinforcements was the women's chorus at the opera house – and it was scarcely thinkable that they should mix with the pupils. In the end the psalm was given up.

A main reason for this problem was that nearly all the pupils, boys and girls, came from 'the less well-off social classes', as the director of the Venice conservatory put it in his 1901 report. Just because they were the children of artisans, shopkeepers and clerical workers they needed to safeguard their respectability.

The Napoleonic rules laid down for the conservatories at Milan and Naples deliberately broke with the old Italian tradition of musical orphanages; pupils paid fees, though there were some free places and scholarships. At Naples, castrated boys (who had earlier been treated as honorary orphans) were banned; in any case they were fast disappearing. The Napoleonic government was also keen to do away with the school's old clerical associations; pupils were no longer to perform at church functions, and their uniform was now to be not ecclesiastical but a semi-military blazer with a lyre on the collar.

Elsewhere the tradition went on. At Parma the school grew out of the orphanage; boys who sang treble got a special diet (as young castrati had in the past) but when their voices broke they had to go back on the normal orphanage diet; when girls' classes were started in 1833 the external pupils from ordinary families in the town had to be kept separate from the orphans. In various southern towns, Naples included, boy inmates of the municipal orphanage were trained to play wind instruments so that they could find places in military or other bands; but, as a recent study of the school at Reggio Calabria has shown, there was a standing temptation to take on external, sometimes paying pupils, to start singing and string instrument classes, and to subordinate everything to the needs of the local opera season. Even though the Ministry of the Interior in Naples rained down instructions to cut down the teaching and go back to training orphans as bandsmen, the school, with the collusion of the municipality, for several years in the 1830s faked its budget and carried on as before.

The Napoleonic conservatories did not go much beyond the old eighteenth-century schools in giving pupils a general as well as a musical education. The report that recommended setting up the Milan conservatory talked of pupils reading 'a few history books' and 'a few treatises on the fine arts'. The purpose of the school was still to train musical craftsmen (and women) while doing away with the old churchy, paternalistic atmosphere. But the spirit of the age got to work; the history of the conservatories through the nineteenth century and well into the twentieth was one of the successive reforms of the curriculum, nearly all aimed at broadening the pupils' education and getting them to experience literature, philosophy, even mathematics and science. For that matter, some people in Italy still complain today that the syllabus is too narrowly professional and musicians come out lacking in general culture.

What is one to make of this? A syllabus is one thing and pupils' actual experience is another. In Italy perhaps even more than elsewhere, a great deal depended on the enthusiasm and concord of the teaching staff. Conservatories went through violent ups and downs in the reported quality of their teaching; thanks to a succession of gifted teachers the Naples conservatory had an excellent piano school even when its general state was deplorable. My own limited experience (in Britain) suggests that the 'general culture' part of their syllabus is apt to make little impression on music students, whatever the hours allocated, partly because so much of students' time and attention is taken up by instrumental practice and partly because music itself is an all-demanding mistress. Of the great twentieth-century conductor Victor de Sabata, who worked right through the Fascist period, it has been said (by his colleague Gianandrea Gavazzeni) that

He was so possessed by his musical demon that nothing else existed. He lived in his circumscribed, stupendous world, born of his exceptional musical nature. Talking about politics with De Sabata would have been impossible ... It would have been futile to ask him who Mussolini, Goering, and Goebbels really were or what they did. He was completely out of this world, in that sense.

An extreme case, no doubt. But Bellini and Donizetti, to judge from their correspondence, were probably little more aware of anything outside music, the theatre business and their intimate emotions. Singers and instrumentalists, to judge from theirs, were almost exclusively concerned with music and money, a few exceptions apart such as Giuditta Pasta, a friend of intellectuals as well as a strong nationalist. Rossini noticed the march of nineteenth-century civilization enough to detest it. Only Verdi stands out as a musician with strong literary interests – and he had been refused admission to the Milan conservatory. This seeming failure probably took him away from the exclusive company of music students, and gave him time to read and look about him.

What can be said is that many conservatory pupils looked to a career in opera. This is hardly surprising; opera was at the heart of Italian musical life. Even at the Milan conservatory, where the first director, Bonifazio Asioli, was a composer chiefly of instrumental and sacred music and was keen to raise the general level of musical culture rather than to turn out star singers, three-fifths of all the works performed in pupils' concerts down to 1860 were operatic extracts. No wonder Michele Ruta complained of the neglect of concert and sacred music.

Of his other subjects of complaint, choral singing for the masses was a great talking point almost from the moment of unification in 1860. Milan, as usual, led the way; the city council in 1862 started a 'people's civic music school' with two sections: choral singing and wind instrument playing. The stated purpose was to 'bring some refinement to the classes so far deprived of the beneficial effects of moral education'; more practically, the two sections pointed, as usual, towards the opera chorus and the military band. When the council decided to have choral singing taught in ordinary elementary schools, Antonio Ghislanzoni, a well-known member of the Milanese 'dishevelled' group, later the librettist of *Aida*, pointed out, in an 1867 article, the roots of this activity in the French revolution – though, as he admitted, only some time after Waterloo had choral singing been introduced in French, Belgian and Prussian schools. Italy, he declared, absolutely must not fall behind these countries if she was to keep her musical supremacy; besides, choral singing would promote in the young a sense of beauty, keep them away from 'other, less pure stimuli', and bring out in a few individuals a disposition for music.

Teaching elementary schoolchildren to sing meant training teachers; but, as an inspector, Ruta found that in one training college the young women did not know whether they were sopranos or altos, could not read music, and just sang in unison the famous chorus from Verdi's *I lombardi* – which, as it happens, *is* in unison. As time went on, however, classes in choral singing established themselves in the conservatories; at Naples they even became compulsory in 1888, though, Naples fashion, they did not actually get under way until 1896. Since Italian schools have not to this day established a practice of teaching instrumental music or theory, we may assume that many Italians' musical experience stems largely from having been made to sing together at school, and that many late nineteenth-century graduates of music schools went out to teach them how to do it.

How else did ordinary Italians come to hear music and perhaps learn something about it? Some literally overheard it; they hung about the stage door of the opera house during the performance and made out what they could. We have descriptions of people doing this during the Bologna performance of Rossini's *Stabat Mater* in 1842, and in Naples in 1864; the first was a special occasion, the other not; it was, we may assume, a common practice, seldom described just because it was common. This was one way for townspeople who could not afford the price even of a gallery ticket to catch a tune or two; in 1893 some of the Milanese could have overheard some of the tunes from *Falstaff* just before the first performance, for in the gallery queue at La Scala were music students, one of whom had helped to prepare the vocal score, and was rehearsing part of it with his friends.

In a warm climate amateur musicians practised for half the year with the window open. Once the opera craze had got going, thanks to Rossini and his successors, there was a market for all kinds of transcriptions; it reached a grand climax with the 245 arrangements of Verdi's *I lombardi alla prima crociata*, which his publisher issued in the ten years following the first performance in 1843; you could buy the complete opera arranged for string quartet, for other string combinations, for piano 'in the easy style', for soprano and tenor in the key of G throughout, and single numbers made over for cornet, for harp and accordion, and for many other instruments; these too must have been overheard by the successors of the 'men and women servants whistling or carolling the airs from the last opera' whom the visiting Englishwoman Clara Novello noted in 1840. Other channels, already mentioned, were brass band concerts in the squares and parks, performances by street musicians and church services where the music might be more operatic than conventionally sacred. At a wedding on Lake Maggiore in the late 1880s 'Largo al factotum', Figaro's entrance aria from *The Barber of Seville*, was played at the elevation.

All but the last of these examples come from the central areas of large towns; not everyone in a working-class suburb could hear a brass band or overhear an amateur cornet player, still less could a peasant deep in the countryside. By the latter half of the century, however, new instruments and new kinds of music-making were bringing the melodies of the towns closer to the grassroots population.

The barrel organ so familiar to our grandparents (and still more to their grandparents) was really an early form of player piano. Though it was being made as early as 1805 it seems to have come into general use in Italy in the 1840s; Bellini in 1828 rejoiced that tunes from *Il pirata* were being sung in Milanese taverns, but by 1845 the devils' chorus from Verdi's *Giovanna d'Arco* was being ground out by barrel organs. These became an Italian speciality abroad, particularly in England, where a number of family firms in the immigrant district of Clerkenwell made them, and men or boys (often monkeys too) took them round the country. The barrel organ probably did more to spread elementary knowledge of music than anything else before the coming of gramophone records. Once again, this was a townee's entertainment, provided by specialists, however modest. But the accordion was a do-it-yourself instrument, well suited to parties and improvised sing-songs, usable in a country inn as much as in town. Again, it was available early in the century – French, Belgian and Austrian manufacturers were making them by the 1830s – but popular-priced versions awaited the setting up of Italian firms in the 1870s.

Music-making – and music-hearing – spread thanks to another new development during the last third or so of the century, the growth of workers' choral societies and amateur bands. This went hand in hand with the development of mutual aid societies and early trade unions. In 1866, during the war for Venice, the choir of the Società Generale degli Operai (an early general trade union) took part in a benefit for soldiers' families at La Scala, singing a war hymn by a well-known radical politician. There were to be many more such performances, more often held on the societies' premises or in the open than in leading opera houses; they are ill documented, but the staple, as usual, was probably the operatic medley. All this was an affair of the industrializing north and the artisan centre rather than of the south. It was exported by north Italian emigrants to Buenos Aires and Montevideo, where choirs and bands flourished about the turn of the century; one of the best known was recruited from the shores of Lake Como.

Since peasants attended markets, fairs and religious festivals it seems likely that many of them first came into contact with art–music through performances given on such occasions by these amateur groups. Near the end of the century the budding Socialist movement took an active hand in bringing music to the people. With a largely rural population like Italy's, early Socialists were more likely to be organizing peasants than industrial workers. A few of them seized on the 'cowshed theatre' (*teatro da stalla*) which, in the latter half of the century, took puppet versions of operas into the farmyards of the north Italian plain, backed by singers and a small band; they injected into the performance a dose of political commentary. In 1897, the year after Italy's disastrous colonial venture into Abyssinia, a farmyard *Aida* made a decided anti-colonial point.

Just when peasants started naming their children after operatic characters is not clear. Probably it was round about the 1890s. A study of the given names of all citizens of Bologna alive in 1975 (including, therefore, some born before 1900) showed a number called Amneris, Aida, Radames, Desdemona, Otello and Norma; the last two names, in my experience, are also found among Tuscan peasants born about 1900. Among the Bolognese surveyed were some with names like Rigoletto and Iago that might be thought inauspicious; there were Lohengrins and even one L'Hoengrin. (The spelling of this popular opera seems at most times to have been a stumbling-block.) This naming of children favoured strong tragic characters; no one seems to have gone for the gentler inhabitants of *La sonnambula* or *L'elisir d'amore*, though these were as current about the turn of the century as *Aida*, *Otello* or *Norma*.

It was in 1896 that Marconi sent out the first faint radio signal. This and the gramophone record – already invented by that date, but still at a rough early stage – were between them to revolutionize the musical lives of Italian peasants and of everyone else, but not until the twentieth century was well advanced. Meanwhile Italians, like most Europeans and Americans, were at an intermediate stage where a kind of popular music found a wide audience without either being rooted in folk custom or relying on new electrical means of diffusion. In England and the United States this meant sentimental ballads and music-hall songs. In Italy it meant the *canzonetta* or 'little song', almost by definition Neapolitan.

Neapolitan songs are what half the world thinks of as Italian music. Young women in Sweden put candles in their hair on St Lucy's day, a winter festival, and sing 'Santa Lucia'. What the cartoon Italian sings in English language television commercials is likely to be 'O sole mio'. Most hearers probably imagine these songs to be folk music. The story is in fact much more complex.

Eighteenth-century Naples was already conscious of its role as capital of the picturesque. The city was at the height of its fame as a tourist resort. Visitors came not just for the antiquities or the bay or the sun or the volcano but for the sight of the population, most of them ragged, idle, cheerful and with a spice of potential danger (they had made a notorious revolution in 1647; they were to make a still more notorious counter-revolution in 1799). Early Neapolitan comic operas exploited these surroundings: they incorporated local characters using dialect and sometimes the words of folk songs. What they made of the song tunes we do not know; the music of these operas is mostly lost. But there was already an interplay between folk song and art song; in a city where at all economic and social levels theatre was a prime activity, each influenced the other, and by the early nineteenth century it was hard to tell where one ended and the other began.

By then there was a song industry, though at a humble artisan level. The best known of many printers of songs, Francesco Azzolino, issued them as flysheets; in his shop piles of them were held down by stones, but he mostly distributed them by selling them to hawkers at 4 carlini (about 1s 4d or 33 cents) a hundred; an old blind Lisabetta, who with her son's help hawked them along with calendars and almanacs, was let off at 3 carlini a hundred. Azzolino himself wrote lyrics, as did shopkeepers, minor lawyers and army officers; the lyrics dealt not only with love but with local eccentrics, picturesque characters and with new fashions like sea bathing. All these songs had composers, though again how much they took from 'folk' melodies (themselves contaminated by decades of interplay with comic opera) is hard to say. By 1840 there was a weekly collection of songs, named after a famous café singer, Pascariello, and selling at 1 grano (just under an old halfpenny) each, with the printer–publisher taking 40 per cent. By 1850 song sheets, or *copielle*, were often being given away free; advertisements on the back paid for them. (As late as 1954, an old, nearly blind man was selling *copielle* in one of the main squares; if you sang him the tune he could fish out the text.) This period, of around 1850, saw a further growth of educated interest in Neapolitan popular culture; much of our documentation dates from accounts published at that time, often with colourful illustrations.

A decisive change took place some time after Italian unification, at about 1880. Neapolitan song became the dominant form of popular entertainment music; it also became big business.

Several things came together. First, a popular festival in the suburb of Piedigrotta was deliberately revived. Secondly, the local song business grew in size and efficiency and had the methods of modern publicity applied to it. Finally, the foreign (mainly French) genre of *café-chantant* hit Naples, as it did other Italian towns, and served to take Neapolitan song to a new bourgeois public. All this went on in a city that had lost its role as capital of the largest Italian state, that was, in places, being torn down and rebuilt as well as having its distances shrunk by railways and trams. According to a modern scholar, Marialuisa Stazio, the myth of Neapolitan song that was then created served to rescue an identity – 'fragments of an "old-time" soul, synthesized into an image, not always idyllic but at least comprehensible and held within the bounds of known and recognizable characteristics.'

Piedigrotta had, until the fall of the Bourbons in 1860, been a military parade, attendant on a feast of the Madonna, with members of the royal family present. It was revived in 1876, as a feast of eating and drinking – supposedly by a newspaper seller who mobilized all the other newspaper sellers to pay one soldo (one old halfpenny or just over one US cent) a day towards the expenses; but it would be surprising if the *camorra* (the Neapolitan form of the mafia) were not involved. The actual Piedigrotta mattered less than the name, which was then used to cover a multitude of activities elsewhere in the city.

It covered, in particular, the song competitions run by new publishers, especially by Ferdinando Bideri. This printer largely beat the old Naples publishers of art–music out of the song field. By about 1900 he was employing some 50 workers, and publishing over a song a week by authors and composers, many of them under exclusive contract. His machinery was up to date and of good quality and he could do three-colour illustrations. It was Bideri – followed by his rivals – who thought up the 'Piedigrotta' song competitions; his were held in a large variety theatre in the modern part of Naples. Between 80 and 300 or so songs would compete each year; claques and counter-claques struggled for dominance; Bideri twisted the arms of the prize committee to get the desired result; of the 300-lire prize he had announced the author got 11 lire while the rest was absorbed by 'expenses'. Among Bideri's competitors were important outside firms like Ricordi of Milan and Polyphon of Leipzig; the latter cornered a number of Neapolitan composers by paying them a monthly retainer. All the competitions were held in the days leading up to the Piedigrotta *festa* (on the Madonna's birthday, 8 September); newspapers and magazines built up the anticipation and people poured in by special train.

The *café-chantant* brought in a new type of singer, often an ill-trained Neapolitan girl from a poor family; she was known as a *sciantosa* (*chanteuse*) and might take a French-sounding name such as 'Fulvia Musette' or 'Gilda Mignonette'. Legend clustered about this figure, her jewels (mostly paste), her hats, her many-coloured underclothes, her unhappy love life. The reality of the café world had a good deal to do with the *camorra* and its system of patronage and protection money. At the same time Neapolitan comic men-singers made headway in the growing number of variety theatres. All this meant a constant demand for new songs, and their specialization into sub-genres intended for particular markets.

The composers who turned them out, often at high speed, were mostly graduates of the Naples conservatory. The best of them wrote other kinds of ballads and salon music besides Neapolitan songs and two of them, Luigi Denza (composer of 'Funiculi-Funicula') and Francesco Paolo Tosti (composer of 'Marechiaro') ended up in London; Tosti taught both Italian and British royalty. Some of the best Neapolitan songs had words by the dialect poet Salvatore Di Giacomo, a gifted and highly self-conscious artist. His lyrics – dwelling much of the time on the loves, fears and adventures of the poor with those tagged as criminal highlighted – did as much as the music itself to fix the myth of Naples, and of Neapolitan song as the type of Italian popular music. 'O sole mio' is still what visitors, Italian ones included, pay gondoliers to sing as they glide along Venice canals.

8 Italy Europeanized

After the momentous first performances of Wagner's *Ring* at Bayreuth in the summer of 1876, the composer and his wife relaxed on a trip to Italy. At the house of the German ambassador in Rome they heard a young Italian composer called Giovanni Sgambati play a piano quintet of his own; the work, as Wagner's wife Cosima noted, 'genuinely interests R[ichard] and is very remarkable; this accomplished musician is entirely lost and neglected here'.

Sgambati's playing at the German embassy was not a coincidence; he had been a pupil of Liszt, gone to Germany and become an admirer of Wagner's music, which in Italy at this time was only beginning to be known. The Wagners saw more of him; it was Sgambati who ran down Italian music, saying that a lot of it was a *dolce far niente* ('sweet do-nothing'), to which Wagner retorted that a lot of German music was a 'painful say-nothing'. Again, it was Wagner who urged the young man to write an opera; but Sgambati was to remain that uncommon bird, an Italian composer who never wrote for the stage. In the modern residential district of Rome where all the streets are named after musicians he has a thoroughfare of his own (rather short); he is dealt with respectfully in histories of music, but his works are seldom played, and many who have a fair knowledge of the current repertoire, wide as that is, would be hard pressed to say what they sound like.

Sgambati's career was an extreme illustration of the changes that were coming over the Italian musical world in the second half of the century. By his death in 1914 musical Italy was a good deal more like her neighbours, France and Germany, than she had been in his student days. At most, the great Italian public was still under the sway of opera, but a portion of it had taken to orchestral and chamber music; the élite of intellectuals and fashionables had now become persuaded that this was the truly important kind of music, and the more intellectual among the younger composers wanted nothing to do with opera as traditionally understood. Symphony concerts had arrived; Italy had produced several internationally famed conductors of whom one, Arturo Toscanini, was reckoned by some to be the best anywhere – this in an age of conductor-worship unexampled before or since. But it had taken a while to get there. The new composers of the early twentieth century, the Respighis and Casellas, could get a hearing at home and abroad, but the musicians like Sgambati, who did the pioneer work and happened not to be transcendent geniuses, tended to remain names on a street plaque.

Why did musical Italy begin to change after the 1848 revolutions? We have seen the general reasons that led people away from old faiths and local allegiances and towards acceptance of the modern state and of what was seen as European civilization. In music, one specific cause was the need to come to terms with the latest thing in opera – Meyerbeer's Paris historical 'big machines'. They required conductors; once conductors of the modern type were found and began to assert their hold, their influence came together with a number of local initiatives summed up as the 'quartet societies', all of which embodied an interest in non-operatic music, not necessarily in string quartets alone.

When the Italian opera world found its feet again after the economic and political crisis of 1848–53, Meyerbeer's Paris operas were not truly new. *Robert le Diable* went back to 1831, *Les Huguenots* to 1836; only *Le Prophète* was as recent as 1849. But they did not really make their way in Italy until the mid-1850s. It is difficult now to credit the seriousness with which these lumbering Paris grand operas were taken; they appeared to be lessons in history as well as in musical science, with their ballets of ghostly nuns (or bathing beauties or skaters) as an authorized bonus. The Mayor of Bologna, together with the dominant group in the town council, was keen to put the city on the musical map as a place of fearless intellectual endeavour. He arranged for the Teatro Comunale to put on all three big Meyerbeer operas in the autumn season of 1869, and already he was thinking of the next coup – the launching of Wagner on Italy, which took place in the same theatre two years later. Not only Wagner but, at that time, Meyerbeer seemed to be the music of the future, identified with progress and the march of science.

Meyerbeerian grand opera, however, required a conductor. Its orchestral colour effects depended on a band of preferably 80 or even 100 players; there were large choruses and complex ensembles. None of this could work on the old system of divided responsibility, with the chief répétiteur taking rehearsals and the leader in charge of performances. The obvious answer was to have an authoritative conductor, as happened in Paris, responsible for both rehearsal and performance.

Le Prophète was on the bill for the Bologna autumn season of 1860; that was when the first Italian conductor of the new type is reckoned to have taken over a leading orchestra. Angelo Mariani had come up in the usual way, as leader, and had already made a name in Genoa. There he had conducted in 1854 a performance of Beethoven's *Eroica Symphony*, said to be an Italian first; the local critics remarked on what a difficult undertaking it was. Mariani in some ways sounds like a forerunner of Toscanini. He stressed the importance of memory in a conductor; he did not, like Toscanini, conduct without a score, but a performance was for him a re-creation of a work which the conductor must have mastered rather than a run-through. He was austere and enforced rigid discipline; he so disliked 'star personalities' among musicians that he is said to have put off the celebrated trumpeter Gaetano Brizzi by denying him an individual bow after Brizzi had played the solo in the 'Inflammatus' from Rossini's *Stabat Mater* (the work was being given its first performance in Rossini's birthplace).

That kind of attitude may have been needed to jolt Italian

orchestras out of their long-standing, comfortable routine. A quarter-century or so later, the young Toscanini so shook the orchestras of Genoa and Pisa (he insisted on using only the best musicians among them) that they went on strike. On the other hand, the concern which Toscanini and later followers like Riccardo Muti were to show for authentic texts was not yet within the spirit of the times; Mariani was quite prepared to enrich the orchestration of *La sonnambula*, which had come to seem weak, and to alter the rhythm of the dances in Verdi's *Don Carlos* to make them sound more like Meyerbeer.

Verdi himself, Mariani's close friend until the two of them fell into a wretched quarrel for reasons that have never been properly explained, was concerned, in these years, to improve Italian orchestras, especially if they were to perform his own recent works. *La forza del destino* (1862) and *Don Carlos* (1867) were what he called *opere d'intenzioni,* operas with a purpose; they were in fact Paris grand operas on the Meyerbeerian model, built by a man with a far better hold of large musical structures than Meyerbeer ever achieved. But they needed Paris-type orchestras or better, whereas in Italy the middle strings in particular, violas and cellos, were – Verdi complained – a 'lot of dogs', and lack of proper rehearsal made orchestras all but incapable of executing 'delicate things'. He therefore insisted that before La Scala put on these works it should take on a full complement of middle strings, get together an orchestra of 100, and provide enough rehearsal time. He got what he wanted in the Italian premiere of *Aida* at La Scala (1872), prepared under his supervision, and repeated the experience at Parma and Naples. This meant that the senior Italian composer was also an innovator in musical practice, directly influencing not only Mariani but younger conductors and musicians down to Toscanini, who could recall just how Verdi wanted such and such a passage played.

What made a career like Angelo Mariani's possible was the change of feeling summed up in the creation in one Italian town after another of a 'quartet society'. This was not just a small group of friends keen to make music together. It meant a rather larger group of people prepared to listen to instrumental music, not all of it necessarily string quartets. In Turin, where the quartet society was founded under that name in 1866, a group had already started forming 12 years earlier centred on the Marchisio family, which included two sisters, later famous as singers, and two musician brothers. The pieces they performed represented Victorian taste – Beethoven's quintet for piano and winds, a piano trio by Hummel and a sextet by Spohr; Beethoven's quartets did not arrive until the 1880s, and then only the early op. 18 set. In Milan the quartet society got going in 1864 with a performance of the inevitable Beethoven septet. This had as its logical consequence three years later (in the minds of contemporaries for whom instrumental music was not subdivided as it is for us) the first orchestral performance in Milan of a Beethoven symphony – the *Sixth*. Other quartet societies in leading towns were founded about this time, Florence having led the way in 1861.

The same logic that followed up Beethoven's septet with the *Pastoral Symphony* led to the starting up of 'people's concert' series. The requirements for these were, first, a small group of enthusiasts on the committee – generally the same people who made up the quartet societies – and secondly, a conductor rooted in the place who could gradually train an orchestra to play a lot of unaccustomed music; by so doing you could hope to train an audience to understand it as well.

In Turin, where the story of the people's concerts is well documented, they grew out of a charity concert arranged in 1872 to replace an end-of-carnival banquet and masked ball. This was in itself symbolic, for the series of banquets and dances at the end of the carnival season had been the high spot of the social year, but by 1870 they were rapidly fading out of fashion. The organizers also drew inspiration from the popular concerts started in Paris three years earlier by Pasdeloup. The first Turin programme included a Meyerbeer overture and the two *Lohengrin* preludes and wedding chorus. All this meant that Turin, a self-consciously modern, go-ahead city, was doing pioneer work, for *Lohengrin* was literally the latest thing – it had had its Italian premiere only a few months before, and had not yet been heard in the town. The conductor was Carlo Pedrotti, as he was to be for the following 11 years.

The concerts in this particular series went on for a little longer; they ended in 1886, after 64 concerts spread over 14 years. In a number of ways they were characteristic of Italian public concerts for many years to come. They were performed not in a purpose-built concert hall, but in a large modern theatre. The orchestra was, for the most part, the one that played for the fashionable winter season in the main Turin opera house. The concerts had their ups and downs, financial and artistic; some were much better attended than others; each was an occasion on its own, looked forward to and afterwards commented upon in the town. This was and is the main difference between Italian concert life, which remains decentralized and provincial to this day, even in Milan or Rome, and the endless routine concert life of London with its multiple orchestral programmes, Mozart and Beethoven and Brahms and Mahler expertly read through, week in week out. A concert, in Italy, remains an event.

We do not hear a great deal about the audience for the Turin concerts. As these were held in the afternoon, they were automatically less fashionable than evening opera performances, and the lowest price (fifty cents for the second gallery, about four old pence) was about half the lowest price for the main opera season. This second gallery is said to have held the most enthusiastic part of the audience, including many students.

The early Turin programmes relied heavily on opera overtures, as if to show that in Italy even instrumental music had to be taken from the theatre. The Italian word for 'overture' is *sinfonia*; some members of the audience may have been hazy about the difference between that and a classical symphony, and the organizers were not in a hurry to make the distinction clear, for they reckoned that both orchestra and audience needed a good deal of training: the scherzo from the *Eroica* was thought to be quite enough to be getting on with at first; Beethoven's *First Symphony*, performed in its entirety in the following year, was sugared with performances of Strauss waltzes in the same programme; when, at the twenty-fifth concert, the orchestra ventured on Beethoven's *Second Symphony*, the compiler of the programme note felt the need to defend the work against charges of being too much 'music of the future', 'scientific' and 'abstract'. There probably was such a need; at an early performance of the *Tannhäuser* overture, a local figure prominent in every sense, a very tall lawyer, shouted 'Out with the barbarians!' Besides overtures, the concerts depended a good deal on symphonic poems and on what have come to be known as 'lollipops' – the staple, in fact, of concert programmes everywhere in the western world until the long-playing record familiarized audiences with more demanding stuff: Liszt's *Second Hungarian Rhapsody*, Berlioz's *Dance of the Sylphs*, Saint-Saëns's *Danse Macabre* and *Le Rouet d'Omphale*.

The Turin orchestra under Pedrotti and the equivalent Milan orchestra under Franco Faccio both played at the Paris international exhibition of 1878; they were said to have shown 'brio, thrust, and energy', though less precision than their French and German competitors. In 1884 it was Turin's turn to play host to an international exhibition (a species of gathering for which there was a late nineteenth-century mania). This time the revelation of the concert series was the conductor Giuseppe Martucci.

Faccio and Martucci were both significant figures. Both were composers; recently an attempt has been made to recover Martucci's symphonies for the repertoire as the work of a kind of Italian Dvořák, with what success it is too early to say. Faccio, the slightly older man, was a member of the Milan 'dishevelled' group. He and his fellow-student Arrigo Boito, later the composer of *Mefistofele* and librettist of Verdi's last Shakespearean operas, went on a pilgrimage to Paris and northern Europe and were drastically critical of the Italian composers of the day. Faccio developed quickly as a conductor; his quality is suggested by Bernard Shaw's comment after hearing him conduct Verdi's *Otello* in London (the work he had launched at its first performance): 'the interpretation of Verdi's score, the artistic homogeneity of performance, the wonderful balance of orchestra, chorus, and principals, stamp Faccio as a masterly conductor'. Unfortunately he fell victim to tertiary syphilis, collapsed, and died when just over 50.

Martucci, a Neapolitan, was the son of an impoverished

trumpeter and bandsman. The father, who had many children, exploited young Giuseppe and his sister by bear-leading them as child-prodigy pianists in and around the Naples area; at one point Giuseppe won a boarding place at the Naples conservatory, but his father took him out again for more touring. At 17 years of age Martucci went to Rome and then on to London, where he played with the famous cellist Alfredo Piatti. He made a considerable reputation as a pianist on his own account, playing not just virtuoso pieces but J. S. Bach and Scarlatti, as well as Schumann and Chopin – an advanced repertoire for the 1870s. Then a Naples aristocrat got him to conduct a small orchestra in his palace and this led to the start of a public concert series.

Martucci's best-known achievement was his conducting of the first Italian performance of *Tristan und Isolde*. This was once again at progressive-minded Bologna, in 1888; by that time Martucci had settled down in Bologna as head of the music school and become one of its most influential musical figures. If *Lohengrin* had seemed novel in the 1870s, with only the middle act to represent the Wagner of 'unending melody' that was supposed to be the 'music of the future', the later Wagner was harder still for Italians to take. The prelude to *Die Meistersinger*, given in Turin in 1883, struck many hearers as bizarre. *Tristan* was quickly picked up by D'Annunzio and made a touchstone for decadent literature. But it was Martucci's seriousness and perfectionism as conductor that had got it launched. Toscanini later (1897) conducted it in Turin, using it as the occasion for putting out all the lights in the auditorium – over the protests of an audience unused to this Wagnerian reform; and Italy for a while had a splendid pair of *Tristan* singers, Giuseppe Borgatti and Amelia Pinto, who sang the work in their own language. Eventually, Martucci went back to Naples as head of the conservatory from which his father had taken him away; at his death, in 1909, Siegfried's funeral march was played to an immense weeping crowd, making it clear that even in Italy – though not for long – Wagnerian ideals had at last triumphed.

A career like Martucci's showed how Europeanized the world of Italian music had become, even though he did not, like

Toscanini, spend much of it outside Italy. What he had done was absorb the leading European tendencies in music and annex them for an Italian tradition of craftsmanship allied to passionate energy, *slancio*.

There was a time, especially in the 1870s, when almost any innovative device was put down to *Wagnerismo;* Verdi suffered from this a good deal as superficial critics noticed the recurring themes in *Aida* and decided that the great man had succumbed to an attack of the leitmotivs. (In fact the recurrent themes were little more than signature tunes; they did not begin to be used or developed as Wagner's were.) The true foreign influence through the sixties and seventies was French. After Meyerbeer came the Massenet of big orientalizing confections – *Le Roi de Lahore* and *Hérodiade*, which reached Italy with much success about the turn of the seventies and eighties – then the more intimate, insinuating Massenet of *Manon* and *Werther*. In either vein, Massenet was easier to assimilate than the more individual Bizet, whose *Carmen* opened up the possibility of realistic treatment of low-life subjects more than it suggested a new musical language. It is, all the same, curious to recall the special part that *Carmen* in Italy played for one important individual. Nietzsche was in Turin, with not long to go before his sudden collapse, when he heard *Carmen* and decided that here was the true Mediterranean music, the sharp gesture at once sensual and ascetic that was to be the antidote to Wagner.

Meanwhile, Wagner himself, as we have seen, was beginning to make his way at last, though *Lohengrin* was his only real popular success, along with the usual 'bleeding chunks' in concert performance, the *Ride of the Valkyries, Siegfried's Rhine Journey* and so on; as late as 1922, *Lohengrin* was still earning its local premiere in the ancient town of Chieti, capital of a province in the Abruzzi. Hence those Lohengrins (not always correctly spelt) in the register of births, alongside the Normas and Otellos.

One more foreign musical import, by no means the least influential, even though it had least status, was operetta. It came in with a rush about 1870, and remained popular until the coming of the cinema at about the time of the First World War. Most of it was French and German or Austro–Hungarian, with works like

Lecocq's *La Fille de Mme Angot*, Planquette's *Les Cloches de Corneville* and the Viennese works of Strauss and Millöcker the staples, though there were some native Italian operettas too. The genre was understood to be separate from opera and was put on in a different way, through permanent touring companies headed by a singer–manager, as happened in the Italian theatre with prose plays. It was immensely popular, but whether its musical manners were fully assimilated is another question.

Operetta needed a light touch that was decidedly non-Italian, a lightness made up of charm and the merest insinuation. Italians like a certain obviousness in human behaviour; disreputable women in particular (and operetta traded in the behaviour of women no better than they should be) jolly well ought to look and act disreputable. Hence the chorus girls in large-scale Italian revues, which took over where operetta left off, looked (as I discovered in 1947, happening to see Wanda Osiris's company arrive at the big Trieste theatre) like a cartoonist's notion of a brothel outing, and at the evening performance the same battered-looking, over-made-up women titupped and straggled through a chorus set to a Tchaikovsky tune, with only a remote acknowledgment of the possibilities of ensemble. It is risky to work back from revue to operetta and from the 1940s to the 1890s, but the knowing, at times salacious tone of 1890s press comment on operetta suggests that, if not a stag entertainment, it was a doubtfully respectable one for a good bourgeois to take his wife and mother-in-law to. That, I suspect, in itself lowered the standard of professional competence looked for.

If Gallic frivolity was hard for Italians to compass, the contemporary Gilbert and Sullivan operetta was both unknown and unknowable; to this day it seems unlikely that an Italian audience could make anything of it whatever, if anybody should be so misguided as to put one of the canon before them – and this even though Gilbert and Sullivan is based, in part, on parody of Italian opera. Its Englishness is of the kind that defies even European union.

Yet Italian musicians by the last decade of the century had travelled a long distance into Europe. The 'young school' that came to sudden notice in 1890, thanks to the overwhelming success of Mascagni's *Cavalleria rusticana*, is now thought of as peculiarly Italian, both in its virtues of passion and directness and in its failings. Yet one of the striking things about it was the way it assimilated non-Italian influences.

This was most obvious on the literary side of their work. In the early nineteenth century Italian librettists and composers had ruthlessly turned every kind of literary source, whether Shakespeare, Schiller, Sir Walter Scott, or the latest Parisian boulevard melodrama, into a string of classically structured scenes worked out in equally classical Italian verse. By the 1880s all that had changed. In *Le Villi*, the young Puccini set out that very world of Germanic legend, with unappeased spirits dancing through the night, that had long been resisted in Italy as alien. The slightly older Alfredo Catalani had a positive relish for that kind of Germanic subject – for mermaids, crags, medieval castles, and, in his last and best-known work, *La Wally*, for rugged Alpine innocence overwhelmed by an avalanche. Mascagni himself, to all appearances a blustering Tuscan, chose an exotic Japanese subject before Puccini did; he also drew on Heine, Ouida and the Alsatian novels of Erckmann-Chatrian (whose local colour he did his best to tease out), besides collaborating at one point with D'Annunzio, the leader of the Italian decadent or aesthetic movement, who had previously denounced Mascagni as a 'bandmaster', but was prepared to let bygones be bygones, for a consideration. Giordano and Cilea were just as apt at incorporating picturesque detail of the French revolution (*Andrea Chénier*) or of the eighteenth-century Paris theatre world (*Adriana Lecouvreur*).

Musically these composers all showed that they had picked up a good deal from a variety of sources, especially from the Massenet of *Manon* and *Werther*. From him they learnt to string colloquial exchanges on a tissue of continuous orchestral chatter, and to work up rapid, overwhelming, emotional explosions cunningly written so as not to tax either the singer or the audience's patience too much. Since instrumental music enjoyed new prestige in Italy, each opera from *Cavalleria* on had to have its orchestral intermezzo or interlude. It sounded like *'Wagnerismo'* all over again, but most of these interludes were simple enough strings of tunes; only Puccini, of all this group, dovetailed and combined themes so that his first acts in particular could be called symphonic in their inspiration and development, and in that sense he was the only one to have really learnt from Wagner.

The 'young school' were so commercially successful all over Europe and America, and successful so markedly with those of their works that were inspired by would-be naturalistic studies of low life – the more brutal and violent the better – that for a long time no one could think straight about them. Fauré, for example, could not bring himself to mention *La bohème* or *Tosca* without an expression of bottomless contempt, yet if he had been able to see past the money they made for their author – galling to a man who himself could not afford the time to compose except in the summer holidays – he might have acknowledged that certain pages in them had a delicacy of feeling and execution not so alien from his own. Now that the dust has settled, what seems striking about the music of the 'young school' is its eclecticism. These composers knew enough about non-Italian traditions of music to pick up all kinds of tricks and use them effectively for purposes of the stage. That, no doubt, is why Giordano's work tends to remind one of much Hollywood film music – there is the same ready means at hand, drawn from the store cupboard of late nineteenth-century European music, to express this or that immediate situation.

What the 'young school' lacked, together with everyone else in the world of Italian music near the end of the century (with a single unrepeatable and inimitable exception) was a set of roots in an Italian culture. Or rather it was that the members of the 'young school' reproduced all too clearly both the uncertainties and the knowingness of the Italian educated classes, who were increasingly dependent on other cultures without being able to assimilate them fully. The exception was, of course, Verdi, who in 1893, at the age of 80, astonished everyone by bringing out *Falstaff*. But although *Falstaff* was the culminating point of an Italian line of musical development, that line was very much Verdi's own, a gossamer thread which he had spun and refined out of his own musical past; it did not lend itself to imitation or continuation. Verdi had for years been a commanding but isolated figure, concerned with innovating on his own account while exhorting everyone else to hold to Italian tradition.

Eight days before the first night of *Falstaff* in Milan, Puccini's first real success, *Manon Lescaut*, was launched in Turin. Bernard Shaw, when he heard it in the following year, at once recognized the 'unmistakably symphonic' treatment of the first act: 'the domain of Italian opera is enlarged by an annexation of German territory'. Because Puccini could still write 'catching melodies' Shaw thought he looked 'more like the heir of Verdi than any of his rivals'. But although this was true in the sense that Puccini did not really belong in the 'young school' he had been lumped with, and was, like Verdi, a far more original and fertile musician than his contemporaries, there were also fundamental differences between him and the older composer.

These were not just differences of temperament or of quality. Verdi had come out of an Italian musical craft, artisan-like in its rules and its common practices; he had done more than anyone else to burst the bounds of the craft and bend its means to his own developing uses, but still, all the while, the craft was there in his habits of mind, almost, one might say, in his fingers. Puccini had behind him not so much a craft as the idea of a craft – the four previous generations of Puccini musicians plus Verdi himself – for him to emulate. But in practice he had to make up his own working practices as he went along, with the whole of nineteenth-century European music to draw upon. Since in every respect save musicianship he was a characteristic child of the Italian petty bourgeoisie near the end of the century, this put an enormous burden on his musical discrimination if he was to save himself from the imbalances and lapses of a Mascagni or a Giordano. It suggests just how fine his specifically musical gift was that his work survives as fully as it does. But it also means that Puccini, even more than the aged Verdi, was an isolated figure in the Italian musical landscape.

Far-fetched though it may sound, Puccini, as an Italian musician, had something in common with his near-contemporary Rudyard Kipling as an English writer. Both were of their time, so obviously that hostile critics could dismiss them as types – at once products and spokesmen – of an overblown bourgeois society and an age of instant mass communication. Both had a sado-masochistic vein, mixed with sentimentality, that can still make for queasiness. Both, on the other hand, had extraordinary command of the resources of language – verbal or musical; much of their work delights as cunningly felicitous sound. With those resources, both were able at times to plumb profound human experience, the more effectively because both were open to unconscious promptings. To have given memorable form to sexual love at its most direct and ardent, as Puccini did in *Tosca* and *Madama Butterfly*, is no small achievement; but there is, too, the desolation of the beleaguered individual (the orchestral passage in *Tosca* while Scarpia writes out the safe-conduct, with its repeated catches of the breath), the tinny grotesquerie of a despotism that can none the less betray and kill (the march before and after the execution) – both prophetic of much twentieth-century experience – and a great deal besides. Like Kipling, finally, Puccini was a master cutter of his own work. The one time when he failed to do the job properly, before the first night of *Madama Butterfly* (1904), he quickly did it afterwards; modern productions that open up his cuts merely show what an expert judge he was of what would and would not work on the lyric stage.

In the next generation the critic Fausto Torrefranca was to launch (1912) a fundamental attack on Puccini in the name of bringing Italian music back to what he saw as its true instrumental tradition, descended from the harpsichordists of the eighteenth century and their forerunners. This was, in part, an extreme form of the usual generational clash, in part an attempt to Europeanize Italian music further by making out that it was really good in the way that German music was good, was indeed better; what was more, it ought to be studied through the kind of musicological research that the Germans had worked up, and who should get the first Italian university post in music history but Torrefranca?

Puccini's music survived the attack; it remained at once hugely successful and artistically isolated. But within his lifetime (he died in 1924) neither Puccini's success nor the hankerings of younger musicians after the virtues of a remote past could get the world of Italian music over the lack of self-confidence which it shared with the new Italian society and state.

9 Expansion and Disintegration

'The people have decided to make war on kings', the famous baritone Cesare Badiali wrote in September 1848, 'and unfortunately on theatres as well'. For the opera world the 1848 revolutions were an unmitigated disaster.

To begin with, the theatres were full of patriotic concerts, historical and military tableaux, farces on political themes, anything rather than opera – which in any case was suspect among some of the democrats of the time as a rich man's toy and a distraction from more earnest challenges. Then, as disturbances continued – street riots, sniper fire, the incursions of counter-revolutionary armies – nobody would stir after dark; the theatres might try to go ahead with the usual opera seasons, but they stood empty. Verdi's patriotic opera *La battaglia di Legnano* had a rousing send-off in Rome, where Mazzini's and Garibaldi's republic was still holding out in the first half of 1849, but in Genoa, the impresario to whom the new work was offered at the reasonable price of 2,000 francs for the hire of the score replied that 'the way the times are going it would be impossible to pay 2,000 francs even for a score by God Himself': he fell back on a Donizetti standby which came free of charge. 'No one does anything', the publisher Giovanni Ricordi complained, 'no one pays and everyone says they are hard up'.

When reaction triumphed all over Italy, the classes that had supported opera in the past were in a poor way. They had had to pay forced loans to the various revolutionary governments, whose paper currency, besides, had quickly lost part of its value. The revolutions had in any case grown out of the severe agrarian economic crisis of 1847, accompanied in parts of the country by famine. It took several years for the economy to recover. Since opera depended on patrons who drew most of their revenue from the land, opera seasons suffered even after 'order' had been restored. Verdi's *Rigoletto* of 1851, put on in Venice, one of the worst-affected towns, would not have seen the light there at all if the restored Austrian government had not been determined to keep the opera house open; it provided an extra subsidy for the purpose, and made the town council follow suit. By 1853–4 the opera world was back to its old routine, but in 1859–60 the war of independence and a further series of revolutions meant more trouble.

This time the effects were lasting. Some towns profited from the new political and commercial life of united Italy – Turin, Milan, Genoa, Bologna and eventually Rome. But others lost their status as capital cities, without for many years gaining anything to put in the place of the courts and bureaucracies and the attendant luxury trades that had made them relatively prosperous. This was true of Naples, Palermo, Venice, Florence, Parma and Modena. The educated classes in all those towns had been used to high-quality opera seasons; in some of them the government had deliberately kept prices low, both the price of the best boxes (which did something to keep the aristocracy happy) and the price of entry to the opera house and therefore of standing room (which avoided putting off the type of young officer, student, or ambitious budding lawyer who was liable to be tempted into revolutionary and nationalist movements). Now there was no one with any interest in handing out what had in effect been collective bribes. The price of the best boxes at the San Carlo, Naples, accordingly almost trebled within ten years.

At the same time the new governments of united Italy had to struggle with heavy financial burdens. In 1868 Parliament not only gave up subsidizing the opera houses which united Italy had taken over from the old states; it imposed a ten per cent tax on all theatre takings. The municipalities were handed the task of carrying on with the subsidy if they chose, but they were now elected – even though on a narrow franchise – and opera subsidies based on indirect taxation were unpopular, for they meant that taxes on poor townspeople's food were helping to pay for rich people's pleasures. Subsidies were accordingly often cut and remained controversial.

Matters were made worse from 1873 by a new, long-lasting agrarian depression, which ate away at landowners' incomes. In Venice, where the town was in a bad way because it had lost its economic function and the upper classes were not getting the expected revenue from their estates on the mainland, the Teatro La Fenice failed to open for 11 years out of 24. This had been one of the three leading opera houses in Italy in the days when Bellini, Donizetti and the young Verdi were writing for it; it remained one of the most beautiful of all theatres; but its day was done. This was an extreme case. The quality of opera seasons undoubtedly went down at the San Carlo, Naples, and at Parma and Modena; in Florence the old leading opera house, La Pergola, gave only fitful seasons. On the other hand Milan was now a relatively prosperous, go-ahead, growing place; the town council by and large kept up the subsidy; La Scala was confirmed in its position of leadership.

Though parts of the Italian opera world were in decay, others had entered a phase of almost explosive growth. This started just before the 1848 revolutions and went on for many years afterwards. It reached into areas of the country where previously it had been unknown or seldom heard. The south in particular, which outside Naples and the three chief towns of Sicily had until then known little except locally based touring companies giving comic opera, began to build theatres and put on the standard repertoire. It was never to be as saturated with opera as the north and centre, but from having been a remote hinterland some of its towns began to form part of a normal circuit. The young Caruso's seasons at Caserta, Salerno and Trapani were not distinguished (the last is remembered for his having got inadvertently drunk on the strong local wine and caused pandemonium by singing 'foxes of Scotland' instead of 'destiny of Scotland'), but half a century earlier they would not have taken place at all. Still more remarkable was the coming of modern music to Cerignola, a desperate set of hovels inhabited by labourers who worked (about 100 days a year) on some of the most brutally run extensive wheat-growing estates in the country; there were just enough landowners and professional men in the region to support a brief opera season and to maintain an unknown young music teacher called Pietro Mascagni.

In those regions where opera had already flourished, many new theatres went up from the late 1840s right down to 1914. They were theatres of a new type: many of them were large, intended as commercial speculations by builders who were not noblemen or even particularly respectable. An example is the Teatro Pagliano in Florence (now the Verdi). It was put up in 1853 by Girolamo Pagliano, a failed baritone who had got as far as being hissed at Pistoia and in a minor Florence theatre. He fell back on inventing and marketing an 'elixir of long life made from a hundred herbs'; this he did so successfully that he was able not only to build and run the biggest opera house in town but also to give private opera performances in his own palazzo featuring his favourite prima donna, just like a seventeenth-century nobleman.

There were many more such theatres put up in these years. Some were known as 'politeama', an imprecise term; it signified mostly that the place was very big. Some were built of wood to begin with, some as open-air theatres for daytime performances; within a few years the men who put them up would try to raise more money and roof them over, or rebuild them in cast iron and stone, or both. The new theatres did not, as a rule, have the vast foyers and staircases of the old monarchical and noble houses; space, in a commercial theatre, had to pay its way. Some of these new buildings burned down or were short-lived for other reasons, generally financial. But the upshot was a vast expansion in the number of theatres and of seats within them.

A census of theatres, drawn up in 1871 for tax purposes, showed 940 theatres in 699 towns. Their distribution was heavily skewed towards the north and centre of the country. They were divided into three classes; the first class included only 11 theatres, two of them in the new capital, Rome, and all of them given over to opera, while the third class (881 theatres) included such curiosities as the two theatres in Vellano, a tiny Apennine town clinging to a precipitous slope and inhabited chiefly by stonemasons; one of them seated 70, the other 30; old people in Vellano in about 1970 could recall having attended performances in one or other of these theatres, but neither can ever have been more than occasionally active.

This was when the boom in theatre building had only just got under way. By 1907 a handbook for theatre people listed over 3,000 theatres; not all of them gave opera, but a surprising number did, even if only for part of the year; there were 25 theatres in Milan, 17 in Naples, 16 in Rome – and two in San Giovanni in Persiceto, a small market town a few miles from Bologna, similar in size to, say, Bromsgrove in England, or Danbury, Connecticut. Some of the places listed as having one theatre had fewer than 2,000 inhabitants. A few years later, in 1914 – just as the cinema was beginning to provide tough competition – another yearbook listed 131 towns as having had opera seasons in the previous year; these included Garlasco, a dusty market town in the middle of the Lombard ricefields, Pontelagoscuro, lost in the marshes of the Po delta, Linguaglossa, an agro-town on the slopes of Etna, and Crotone, a bleak little port on the treeless east coast of Calabria.

What was the reason for this explosion of theatre building? There was undoubtedly a new audience – one that had not been catered for in the theatres built by and for sovereign rulers or noblemen, and that had been relegated to a few smoky, cramped old houses in the biggest towns. United Italy remained a poor country, but it was less poor than before; in particular it was growing more urbanized, and that meant new groups of white-collar employees – clerks, shop assistants, minor officials – with a little money to spare for an outing to the opera. Because the new large theatres were not officially subsidized or controlled, they are ill-documented; we know surprisingly little about their day-to-day running. It is, however, clear that they were much more cheaply priced than the old leading opera houses; features like special low prices offered to commercial travellers, or to families who came bringing children under seven, suggest some of the groups they hoped to attract.

What were the performances like? Again, we do not often hear in detail, because such theatres were generally outside the net of cultivated audiences that were held to warrant detailed criticism in the press. The best of the popular-priced theatres may, however, have kept up a good standard at an energetic, rough-and-ready level, perhaps more consistently than some of the old monarchical or aristocratic theatres with their high pretensions which they were no longer always able to finance. Naples critics of the end of the century tended to praise the work done by the large, popular-priced Teatro Bellini at the expense of the apparently more ambitious seasons at the San Carlo. An *Aida* of 1893 at the Bellini, according to one critic, was carefully rehearsed and competently performed. The audience lacked the San Carlo public's

ostentatious reluctance to be roused, its haughty pretension to infallible judgment. But against this there was a mass public, open to impressions, unaware of aesthetic subtleties ... the public that lets itself be swayed by emotion and that, regardless of pressures or schools, loves above all music that excites it.

Another spectacular opera at the Verdi, Florence (formerly the Pagliano), was – Arnold Bennett reported – done competently and on a large scale, with a chorus of 120 and many small shopkeepers in the audience.

When things went wrong in these theatres, however, the audience did not do things by halves. At the Pagliano, a dried cod's head flung at the baritone was all in the day's work; rather more threatening was a bench hurled from the fifth tier that narrowly missed the impresario. At the main Parma theatre – which by this time, like other old royal theatres, gave occasional popular-priced performances, – a dialect poem describes the audience at an early twentieth-century *Otello*, attended by shoemakers, women with bunions, and others from 'across the water' (the working-class district of Parma, where Toscanini came from). All of them have relatives in the chorus:

And when Otello sends out his 'Esultate' with that high note sailing smoothly up, they all go crazy, and stamp their feet to demand an encore'; [but the baritone is a 'dog' and at *his* high notes the people shout] 'It's a disgrace! I'll get you when you're out on the street!

What made these new audiences possible was not just lower prices; it was the coming of repertory opera. Nowadays we are used to the idea that opera houses exist chiefly to put on the same fifteen or twenty operas, the only differences from season to season being new singers or new productions. But in the mid nineteenth century this was a new way of doing things. Until then, people generally expected operas to be new, and if not absolutely new, then new to them. They heard them in much the same spirit as a modern television audience watching a new situation comedy, which no doubt has familiar features but dressed in some kind of new array. The expression 'repertory opera' seems to date from the 1840s, and so does the phenomenon itself. From then on, and especially from about 1860, repertory opera became the norm.

The repertory was highly selective. By 1913 it included very few works earlier than *Rigoletto* (1851). The small band of older survivors included *The Barber of Seville*, *Norma*, *La sonnambula*, *L'elisir d'amore*, *Lucia di Lammermoor*; all these achieved a surprising number of performances. They were followed by *I puritani*, *Don Pasquale*, *Linda di Chamounix*, *La favorita*, *Ernani*, and Auber's *Fra Diavolo*, with rather fewer. But the other works of Rossini, Bellini, and Donizetti, and Verdi's early works other than *Ernani*, had virtually disappeared. The operas that did get put on year in year out were Verdi's later works, Ponchielli's *La Gioconda*, a number of French operas (several by Massenet and Thomas, plus *Faust* and *Carmen*) and, by 1913, the successful works of Puccini and the 'young school'. There were still some new operas being put on by Italian composers; in that year, 28 were listed (12 of them in one act) of which only Montemezzi's *L'amore dei tre re* is now remembered. But that was nothing to the output of the eighteenth or the early nineteenth century.

One reason for the smaller number of new operas was that, since the coming of effective copyright, a successful opera had become big business. It represented 'capital', as a critic writing in

1882 pointed out: 'you can make tens of thousands [of francs], and if its artistic value rises above the common level it can bring in as much as a large estate'. Such a potentially valuable property must be worked on with great care; it could no longer be turned out in a hurry on the old journalistic system followed by nearly every composer up to the young Verdi.

The mid-century taste for Parisian grand opera, and the general cult of size and elaboration in the arts, worked the same way: 'every beardless boy just out of school', another critic wrote in 1878, 'wants to write not a comic opera but a grand opera with knobs on, in five acts, with ballets, a triumphal march, and the inevitable conspiracy ...' He may have been thinking of Stefano Gobatti's *I Goti* (1873), a beginner's work that had a flash-in-the-pan success when enthusiastically promoted by the composer's fellow-Bolognese; but there were plenty more. By the 1890s, the influence of D'Annunzian aestheticism made sheer size for its own sake seem vulgar, though there was still plenty of room for lush sets, costumes, language and emotions.

The people who had most to gain from a lasting hit were now, apart from the composers themselves, the publishers. They would receive payment every time the score of a successful opera was hired out to one of the 150 or so Italian opera houses, to say nothing of royalties abroad and sales of sheet music. No wonder they nurtured 'their' promising composers; Giulio Ricordi, head of the Milan firm, subsidized Puccini for nine years until the composer broke through with *Manon Lescaut.*

The rise of publishers, like that of large popular-priced opera houses, was bound up with the coming of repertory opera; there was a lot more money to be made from hiring out the score and parts of the same successful work than from publishing one new work after another. In the 1850s the leading Italian music publishers started putting out production books for local opera companies to follow, along with sketches of sets and costumes; by the 1860s they were deciding not only which opera should be done in which theatre but also who should sing in it.

The remainder of the century saw a series of battles between two or three publishers (Ricordi, Lucca – absorbed by Ricordi in 1888 – and Sonzogno) over the works of popular composers and the control of key theatres, La Scala in particular. Ricordi had Verdi in his stable and then Puccini. The widowed Signora Lucca – a large, vital woman who had always overshadowed her husband even when he was alive – had Wagner; the composer, who liked her fearless advocacy, declared that nature had intended to make a man, 'but, seeing that the men in Italy were not up to much', had changed her mind. Sonzogno had Mascagni, a number of key works by French composers and a keen eye for publicity; he invented the gimmick of the multiple premiere, although seven simultaneous first nights did not prevent Mascagni's *Le maschere* from being a flop.

When the publisher was in charge of every significant detail, the impresario dwindled into little more than an executant. Even the more enterprising ones now found that they could exert little initiative; the impresario of the old Turin royal theatre, who successfully introduced Massenet to Italy, was to have had the composer's next new work, but could not get it because the publisher chose to have it put on in Milan instead. The economic crisis that hit so many of the older opera houses made the impresario's business still more precarious. Singers, at times, insisted on being paid before the last act of every performance and more impresarios than in the past turned into literally fly-by-night operators; one Rome impresario, hard pressed by his creditors, invited them to meet him after the last performance of the season, but meanwhile collected the night's box-office takings and fled over the roofs.

The one field where Italian impresarios could still work on a large scale was South America, especially the network made up of the chief cities of Argentina, Uruguay, Brazil and Chile. By the 1870s these had a prosperous local ruling class – its wealth built up from the export of food and raw materials to Europe, and its members keen on European culture – as well as a strong Italian immigrant presence. Copyright took longer to establish itself in this part of the world than elsewhere; Italian publishers could not have their own way unopposed as they did at home. A year after the first performance of Verdi's *Otello*, there were rival versions mounted in the two leading opera houses of Buenos Aires, each put on by a locally based Italian impresario with one of the two most renowned Otellos anywhere (Francesco Tamagno and Roberto Stagno), one authorized by Verdi's publisher, the other a pirated version. Down to the First World War it became normal practice for Ricordi in Milan to send out to South America an entire opera company, complete with sets, costumes, chorus, and stagehands, all of them recruited in Italy, basically from La Scala. At the same time a rival Italian company, even two rival companies in certain years, would be competing with the Ricordi company in other South American theatres. The tenor Beniamino Gigli, who went out as a young man with one of these companies, recalled how they and their rivals fraternized while on the fortnight's steamer voyage but were then forbidden to speak to each other the moment they sighted land.

Rich as this South American territory was, it remained, for the time being, a straightforward export market for Italian opera; the Americas as yet created little opera of their own. One of Sonzogno's gimmicks was to give the first performance of Mascagni's *Isabeau* (1911) in Buenos Aires, but it was rehearsed in every detail before the company embarked, and was even allowed a 'dress rehearsal' at Genoa for the benefit of Italian critics. North America, where Puccini's *La fanciulla del West* had its first performance in the previous year, had a large Italian immigrant population, but there it had to reckon with an earlier German influence and with the cosmopolitan tastes of the educated élite.

The coming of repertory opera made a difference to singers more than to any other group of musicians. Until the mid nineteenth century they had had to learn their parts quickly, but each new opera had been preceded by a period of rehearsal, however feverish. Now every singer had his or her repertory of established operas, to be performed with one or two rehearsals or none.

This was not a wholly new idea. Eighteenth-century singers had often been identified with certain parts – Metastasio's Dido, say – but had performed them in versions set by different composers in turn. One or two famous singers about the turn of the eighteenth and nineteenth centuries built up international careers by specializing in a few parts that showed them at their best: Crescentini as Romeo (in Zingarelli's opera) among other roles, Giuditta Pasta as Romeo (again), as Mayr's Medea, and as Rossini's Tancredi and Desdemona. But that was a matter of refining and deepening a few interpretations. The new repertory system meant that singers had to have a whole battery of parts more or less at their command.

The baritone Giovanni Marchetti was shocked in 1866 to discover that he was expected to sing up to 18 parts in a Constantinople season. But in 1902 the bass Vittorio Arimondi signed a contract detailing 39 parts which he must be ready to perform in South America; these ranged from Leporello to Hunding and King Mark by way of coloratura bass parts in *I puritani* and *Lucrezia Borgia*. A mere 18 parts was, by then, regarded as a normal drop-of-a-hat repertoire. Even then, Italy never went as far as the German opera world, where the same artists sang opera and operetta. There – according to the famous singing teacher Mathilde Marchesi, writing in 1889 – one soprano had a repertoire of 54 parts, and might be required to learn one more within three days.

Under the new system, leading singers could choose the opera in which they would make their first appearance of the season (with, as they hoped, maximum impact on the audience); by about 1870 this had developed into an absolute right. The results could be unfortunate, as a man experienced in the management of La Scala pointed out:

... the opera chosen by the prima donna fails to please the tenor or the baritone: the tessitura is too high or too low, or the part isn't conspicuous enough, so they won't accept it; and contrariwise the début arranged by the tenor doesn't suit the soprano or the bass, who appears only in the third act – there's only an aria and a duet for him – the part is a mere trifle – a self-respecting artist can't possibly accept it. And so on.

A further problem was that singers did not want to share a part with a colleague appearing in the same season; yet the repertory system made it easy and often attractive for them to contract for only a few performances at a time. It mattered not whether the other singer was to precede or follow; Maddalena Mariani Masi's 'delicacy as an artist' told her not to follow the celebrated Teresa Stolz as Aida, while the Spanish tenor Francisco Viñas would not appear in Rome if his part was to be sung later in the season by Francesco Marconi, a native Roman whom the audience was likely to take to its heart. This kind of 'delicacy' was to plague managements into the twentieth century. Rather than mere whim, it was a legacy from the old arrangement of fixed seasons, in which individual artists hoped to impress a local audience in a part they could make their own; but it became more and more outdated. Some managements tried to guard against it in contracts; it was eventually forbidden by the Fascist Government in 1932.

Repertory opera all too often meant that performances were flung on to the stage. Managements might not know a few weeks before the start of the season which operas they were to put on; the programme was then made up from week to week (not only in Italy but, up to 1908, at the Metropolitan in New York), sometimes from day to day. Four performances of *Otello* at La Fenice, Venice, in 1892 saw two Otellos and two Desdemonas, all of them last-minute replacements; the performances were not a success. Singers arrived with their own costumes and their own set routine; even at La Scala, before Toscanini took the place in hand, you might see 'a love duet sung from opposite ends of the stage, because the tenor was used to singing that scene downstage right and the soprano, unfortunately, downstage left'. The baritone Francesco Graziani, writing to his agent from Moscow in 1874, excused himself for not having written sooner:

... until today I've worked like a dog [literally 'like a customs man's donkey'], three or four performances a week, but that's nothing with *Hamlet* on my back, plus a bit of *Don Pasquale*, which I've never done before; imagine whether I had time even to wash my balls. I'd forgotten the best part – rehearsals for eight operas ...

There is little doubt that standards of performance, by and large, deteriorated in the half-century or so up to the First World War. It was an age of great singers; many of them, however, spent most of their careers singing outside Italy, and when Toscanini did take La Scala in hand (from 1898), the great baritone Titta Ruffo strongly disliked having to submit to a fortnight's rehearsal, including three orchestral rehearsals sung in full voice, costume, and make-up: 'I could with an easy conscience have faced the La Scala audience after one piano and one orchestral rehearsal' – so Titta maintained even a quarter-century later, when Toscanini's reforms were beginning to be generally accepted.

The general expansion of opera also meant that many indifferent singers could make some sort of career. Singers who in 1896–7 were on the books of Milan theatrical agencies totalled 1,106, nearly all Italians; they included 371 sopranos and 270 tenors. The Milan agents themselves numbered 26, and the same directory listed 33 private singing teachers (plus six teachers of declamation and dramatic art). A little earlier, in 1889, the publisher Giulio Ricordi had estimated that some 3,000 people in Milan earned a living from opera and ballet, to say nothing of those who lived off the tourist trade which opera helped to stimulate.

What Ricordi did not say was that many of these people lived from hand to mouth. Already in the 1850s, as the Italian-trained baritone Charles Santley recalled, struggling artists might have to perform when driven literally 'to the confines of starvation'. Matters were, if anything, worse later in the century; at Assisi in 1889 a principal tenor was expected to sing for 6 francs (4s 10d) a night – and that was during carnival, the most favourable season because the busiest.

There was even competition from troupes made up of pre-pubertal children. These were in vogue from about 1870 until the First World War. The teacher–impresarios who ran them exploited the Italian version of a late nineteenth-century European and American craze for 'cute' child performers; they gathered up children from families where a breadwinner was needed, coached them, and took them round Italy, eventually round the Americas. The troupes performed mainly comic opera, but from 1904 one at least put on *Lucia*, *Rigoletto* and *La traviata* with all the parts sung in the treble clef; its diminutive lead singer, Arnaldo Tedeschi ('*Il piccolo Tamagno*') was billed as six years old (he was then nine) and would sing 'Di quella pira' from *Il trovatore* between the acts of comic operas. Neither he nor any other member of these companies is known to have gone on to an adult singing career; meanwhile they seem to have earned more than a child could have made in other occupations. In the period of Giolittian liberalism from 1900, Italian public opinion began to turn against the exploitation of child labour; this, as much as anything, seems to account for the disappearance of the troupes. The last one heard of was in Brazil in 1920.

Cut-rate foreign competition was a further hazard. The young Santley had paid for his lessons and gone on to earn modest fees from engagements at Pavia and elsewhere, competing on equal terms with Italian singers of his own age. But from the 1860s a stream of young, foreign aspirants, mainly British or American women, were willing to appear in Italy for nothing, or even to pay managements for the privilege; it was supposed to be good experience as well as a suitable advertisement back home.

The great North-American sopranos Emma Albani (Marie Lajeunesse) and Lillian Nordica (Norton) began in this way (at Messina and Brescia in the 1870s), but they at least were good enough not to have to pay for a début. Others did, Italians included: Leonilda Diotti, a young married woman, by 1883 had made 'many sacrifices' with her husband's consent to study singing, but when it came to an opera début she found she would have to pay; her husband could not manage it; she took sulphuric acid and killed herself. A Milan journal commented: 'The barbarian invasion from beyond the ocean and the Channel, even from beyond the Alps ... has made middling women artists' situation still more appalling, and newcomers' first steps still more difficult'. In 1911 the minor coloratura soprano Meta Reddish, from upstate New York, heard a cry of 'Down with Americans!' from the San Carlo gallery as she made her début (in a single performance, after a single offstage piano rehearsal). She had not had to pay the management; she had however made the usual contribution, at a specially arranged low rate of 50 lire (£2 or US $10), to 'a man about 40, dark and thick-set and fairly well dressed' as well as polite – the representative of the *camorra*, the Naples version of the mafia.

At the same theatre in the previous year a performance of

La traviata had shown the repertory system at its worst. It had been put on in a hurry because the great baritone Ricardo Stracciari was unexpectedly available. But, Stracciari apart, nothing worked. According to a contemporary journal,

The scenery was old, the so-called modern costumes seemed to have come from an old-clothes shop...The chorus...were dull, disorderly, colourless and seemed not to care. The orchestra endured the performance, without spirit, without application, without emotional impulse...After protests and disputes that seemed likely to bring matters to a tragic end, the thing turned to comedy. People coughed, talked aloud, laughed at the doctor, laughed at the costumes, laughed at the fourth act. And there may have been laughter backstage as well, for the hullabaloo there could be distinctly heard in the auditorium.

Later in the season, at a cut-price performance given for people attending a congress, the celebrated Cleofonte Campanini was announced as conductor, but in the event a young substitute beat time from a vocal score.

On the other hand, even an ill-prepared performance might catch fire from the emotional energy of the singers – what Italians called *slancio*, i.e. throwing yourself into it with everything you have. Diaghilev once expressed his admiration for a *Ballo in maschera* at Perugia in which, as he put it, nothing got in the way of the singing. That was not the principle he followed in his own ballet stagings where the sets and costumes mattered at least as much as the dancing; still, what he meant will be clear to anyone who has been caught up in the exhilaration of an Italian opera performance at once semi-improvised and blessed – a kind increasingly rare.

The audience in the years after unification was also able to let go in a way that had been hampered by the police regulations of the old despotic states. Now that you could no longer have obstreperous members of the public arrested, those who disliked the performance for any reason could hiss unrestrained. A *Linda di Chamounix* at Voghera in 1875 ran through four tenors in ten days because the first three were hissed, one of them literally off the stage; the performance had to go on without him or any other tenor. (The Voghera audience in these years was said to be tolerant of weak voices but merciless to anyone who sang out of tune.) A disastrous Musetta, in *La bohème* at Vicenza in 1913, 'while taking a high note was so hissed that ... she was quite overcome and was unable to close her mouth, it having been stretched from ear to ear'; a doctor later closed it with difficulty.

If the audience raised a persistent storm of boos and hisses there was nothing for it but to lower the curtain and stop the performance. Trouble was particularly likely in former capitals where standards since unification had dropped. Of these, Parma was the most notorious, thanks also to its citizens' view of themselves as high-tempered eaters of salami and meat. There were serious disturbances there in 1865, 1870, 1872, 1878, 1879, 1882 and beyond; in most of those years performances were stopped, sometimes before the end of the first act, and on two occasions the row was such that prima donnas fainted on stage. The Parmesans liked to think of themselves as connoisseurs. They were certainly connoisseurs of *acuti* – the loud high notes that were now the surest passport to applause.

Opera was now on the way to becoming a spectator sport. For much of the nineteenth century it had been something more – at its best, an art created through a close interplay between musicians and audience, phrase by phrase, even note by note. That kind of responsive listening flourished in a society with few other entertainments. But by the early twentieth century opera had many non-musical competitors. Not only were there now many newspapers, magazines and novels; Italy was a pioneer of silent cinema – it vied with California in the production of epics even before the outbreak of the First World War. Radio, a partly Italian invention, was in the offing; between the wars professional football was to become a craze. Opera on the old scale could not stand up to the competition.

In Milan in 1918 three leading theatres were putting on opera simultaneously; with the help of matinees, they gave, within ten hours, three operas by Verdi and two by Mascagni. But that kind of largess was probably never repeated, for the end of the First World War signalled the overwhelming success of film as a popular entertainment. Within a few years it was to take over many former opera houses.

All the same, habit died hard. In the small town of Bagnacavallo, near Ravenna (known to English-speaking readers as the place where Byron's little daughter, Allegra, died), the trade fair season in the 1850s had normally brought 18 performances divided between two operas. As late as 1928 it still managed ten performances of one opera. In the south, late as usual in registering social change, the old rickety seasons managed by impresarios lingered on into the 1950s. At the opposite extreme, Milan, the pioneer in introducing modern methods of opera production (and nearly every other innovation), has never quite lost the old feeling for opera as the currency of civic life and of private gossip alike. All the same, there can be no doubt that in the second half of the twentieth century the true musical hero of most Italians is not Pavarotti but the latest successor to Elvis Presley.

Further Reading

These suggestions are intended for English-speaking readers. They do not constitute a bibliography; to tackle the subject comprehensively one must go to Italian sources. The book rests in part on my previous work on the social history of opera, itself based on research in mainly Italian archives; in part on the largely Italian literature on other aspects of nineteenth-century musical life; and a little on personal experience. In what follows I have mentioned the most indispensable Italian sources, while concentrating on useful and interesting reading in English.

The archives I have used fall into two main kinds: government papers, which in pre-unification Italy took a close interest in music and especially opera; and the correspondence of impresarios and musicians. I have worked mainly in the archives of Paris, Milan, Venice, Parma, Bologna, Lucca, Rome and Naples, but these are far from exhausting the available documentation. Correspondence can be found in many places. The most important collections open to the public are: the Museo Teatrale alla Scala/Biblioteca Livia Simoni, Milan; the Collezione Piancastelli in the Biblioteca Comunale, Forlì; the Fondo Pacini in the Biblioteca Comunale, Pescia; and the Biblioteca Nazionale, Florence (two collections of Alessandro Lanari's papers). Among printed sources I have used Italian-language histories of individual theatres and of conservatories, as well as journals and directories – far too many to list; also Spanish and Portuguese sources on Italian musicians in Latin America.

There is no general work on the subject defined by the title of this book. Recent general histories of Italy are S. J. Woolf, *A History of Italy 1700–1860* (London, 1979) and Martin Clark, *Modern Italy*

1871–1982 (London, 1984). Culture and entertainment in the latter part of the 'long nineteenth century' are dealt with in D. Forgacs, *Italian Culture in the Industrial Era, 1910–80* (Manchester, 1990). The six-volume *Storia dell'Opera Italiana* (ed. L. Bianconi and G. Pestelli, Turin, 1987–   ), which reflects recent interest in social history and is still in course of publication, is to be issued in English translation by the University of Chicago Press. Meanwhile there are useful articles in *The New Grove Dictionary of Music and Musicians* (6th ed., ed. S. Sadie, London, 1980) and there will be new ones in its offshoot *The New Grove Dictionary of Opera* (due about 1992).

On opera, the field best covered by English-speaking writers, the reader would do well to start with the general chapters in each of the three volumes of J. Budden, *The Operas of Verdi* (London, 1973–81), and with E. J. Dent, *The Rise of Romantic Opera* (ed. W. Dean, Cambridge, 1976). The business and organizational side of opera is dealt with in my *The Opera Industry in Italy from Cimarosa to Verdi. The Role of the Impresario* (Cambridge, 1984) and in parts of M. Chusid and W. Weaver (eds), *The Verdi Companion* (London, 1980); for Latin America, see my 'The Opera Business and the Italian Immigrant Community in Latin America, 1820–1930: the Example of Buenos Aires', *Past and Present*, no. 127 (May, 1990). An extraordinarily detailed dossier of the creation of a Verdi opera is H. Busch, *Verdi's Aida: the History of an Opera in Letters and Documents* (Minneapolis, 1978); Busch has since (1989) done the same job on *Otello*. A penetrating analysis of the workings of censorship is M. Lavagetto, *Un caso di censura: il 'Rigoletto'* (Milan, 1979).

On individual opera composers, the best studies are R. Osborne, *Rossini* (London, 1986), W. Ashbrook, *Donizetti and his Operas* (Cambridge, 1982), J. Budden, *Verdi* (London, 1985), G. Baldini, *The Story of Giuseppe Verdi* (Cambridge, 1980), F. Walker, *The Man Verdi* (London, 1962), M. Carner, *Puccini* (London, 1958), and E. Greenfield, *Puccini: Keeper of the Seal* (London, 1958). Julian Budden's study of Puccini is something to look forward to. There is nothing really satisfactory in English on Bellini; his *Epistolario* (ed. L. Cambi, Milan, 1943) is the fundamental source. The only conductor to have been studied at book length in English (by H. Sachs) is *Toscanini* (London, 1978).

Books by musicians who worked in Italy include, among singers, the vivid autobiography of Charles Santley, *Student and Singer* (London, 1892), the unknown but illuminating Francis Walker,

Letters of a Baritone (London, 1895), and the scarcely better-known *Lillian Nordica's Hints to Singers* (ed. W. Armstrong, New York, 1923), which includes the singer's and her mother's letters home; see also A. Mackenzie-Grieve, *Clara Novello* (London, 1955) and the unintentionally hilarious (and revealing) C. Reddish, *A Chronicle of Memories* (Miami, 1950). I hope Kenneth A. Stern will soon bring out a biography of Giuditta Pasta (based on his 1984 Ph.D. thesis at the City University of New York) and William Seward one of Adelina Patti; Michael Henstock has published a very full study of Fernando De Lucia (London, 1990). From an earlier period, the *Reminiscences* of Michael Kelly, a tenor who worked with Mozart (ed. R. Fiske, Oxford, 1975), are entertaining though occasionally unreliable in detail, while, for the early twentieth century, Rosa Ponselle and J. A. Drake, *Ponselle: A Singer's Life* (Garden City, 1982) – several cuts above the run of singers' (auto)biographies – tells one much about the Italo–American musical world.

Testimony by other musicians or musical hangers-on includes the direct evidence of the musicologist Charles Burney in *Music, Men, and Manners in France and Italy, 1770* (ed. H. E. Poole, London, 1969) and *A General History of Music* (ed. F. Mercer, London, 1935); the *Memoirs* of Lorenzo da Ponte (ed. and transl. E. Abbott, New York, 1929) and the *Life of Rossini* by Stendhal (ed. and transl. R. N. Coe, London, 1956) – both unreliable but good on atmosphere; *The Letters of Mozart and his Family* (ed. E. Anderson, revised version, London, 1985); Louis Spohr's *Autobiography* (London, 1865); the *Memoirs* of Hector Berlioz (ed. and transl. D. Cairns, London, 1975); *Giacomo Meyerbeer: his Life as seen through his Letters* (ed. H. and G. Becker, Portland, Oregon, 1989); and the sparkling criticism of George Bernard Shaw, collected in *London Music in 1888–89* (London, 1937), *Music in London 1890–94* (London, 1932), and *How to become a Musical Critic* (ed. Dan H. Laurence, London, 1960) (and now in *Shaw's Music*, ed. Laurence, London, 1989). Works by two British theatre managers who dealt in Italian opera are J. Ebers, *Seven Years of the King's Theatre* (London, 1828) and *The Mapleson Memoirs* (ed. H. Rosenthal, London, 1966).

There are many observations by foreign travellers, often superficial and repetitive; four that stand out are J. W. Goethe, *Italian Journey* (transl. W. H. Auden and E. Mayer, London, 1962), Hester Lynch Piozzi, *Observations and Reflections made in the course of a Journey through France, Italy, and Germany* (London, 1789), Sydney Owenson, Lady Morgan, *Italy* (London, 1821), and, for a few memorable nuggets, *The Gladstone Diaries* (ed. M. R. D. Foot and H. C. G. Matthew, Oxford, 1968–).

On folk song the standard work is R. Leydi, *I canti popolari italiani* (Milan, 1973); on Neapolitan song, S. Di Massa, *Storia della canzone napoletana* (Naples, 1961), with M. Stazio, *Parolieri e paroliberi* (Naples, 1987) a stimulating reinterpretation and the older F. de Bourcard (ed.), *Usi e costumi di Napoli e contorni* (Naples, 1857, 1866; reprint Naples, 1976) a fertile and well-illustrated source.

On instrumental music there is little in English apart from articles in *The New Grove*. S. Martinotti, *Ottocento strumentale italiano* (Bologna, 1972) is a general treatment; G. Depanis studies Turin in *I concerti popolari e il Teatro Regio di Torino* (Turin, 1914–15) and M. De Angelis Florence in *La musica del Granduca* (Florence, 1978). Antonio Bazzini, a crucial figure, is dealt with in C. Sartori, *L'avventura del violino* (Turin, 1978). Marion S. Miller's essay on 'Wagner, Wagnerism, and Italian Identity' is in D. C. Large and W. Weber, *Wagnerism in European Culture and Politics* (Ithaca and London, 1984). Information on church music, a largely unknown field, has to be gleaned here and there; but see M. Girardi and P. Petrobelli (eds), *Messa per Rossini. La storia, il testo, la musica* (Parma/Milan, 1988).

Music publishers and their influence have not been satisfactorily studied in any language. L. Jensen, *Giuseppe Verdi & Giovanni Ricordi, with Notes on Francesco Lucca* (New York and London, 1989), collects much fascinating information.

Education and training have to be studied in specialized monographs. Two good studies in English of important institutions that just preceded our period are M. F. Robinson, 'The Governors' Minutes of the Conservatorio S. Maria di Loreto, Naples', *RMA Research Chronicle*, X (1972), and M. V. Constable, 'The Venetian "Figlie del Coro": their Environment and Achievement', *Music and Letters*, LXIII (July–October 1982).

Index